WITNESSES TO THE
HOLOCAUST

STORIES OF MINNESOTA HOLOCAUST SURVIVORS AND LIBERATORS

Number and Percent of Jewish Population Murdered in the Holocaust*

NORTH SEA

BALTIC SEA

ADRIATIC SEA

MEDITERRANEAN SEA

BLACK SEA

NORWAY
900/50%

ESTONIA
1,000/40%

HOLLAND
106,000/75%

LATVIA
80,000/90%

LITHUANIA
135,000/90%

GERMANY
210,000/88%

POLAND
3,000,000/90%

BELGIUM
40,000/60%

SOVIET UNION
1,000,000/60%

LUXEMBOURG
1,000/20%

AUSTRIA
65,000/88%

CZECHOSLOVAKIA
217,000/83%

FRANCE
90,000/25%

HUNGARY
450,00/70%

ITALY
8,000/20%

ROMANIA
300,000/50%

YUGOSLAVIA
60,000/60%

GREECE
65,000/77%

N

Europe in 1942	
———	German Border
—·—·—	International Border
- - - -	Furthest Eastern German Advance

Miles
0   100   200   300
0   200   400
Kilometers

* Estimated

WITNESSES TO THE HOLOCAUST

STORIES OF MINNESOTA HOLOCAUST SURVIVORS AND LIBERATORS

25th Anniversary Edition

EDITED BY LAURA ZELLE AND
JONI SUSSMAN

Edited by Laura Zelle and Joni Sussman

Portrait photography in this book appears courtesy of David Sherman Photography
www.davidshermanphoto.com, created as part of Transfer of Memory,
The Minnesota Holocaust Survivor Portrait Project www.transferofmemory.org

War era photos and cover photos appear courtesy of Holocaust survivor families

For information
Jewish Community Relations Council of Minnesota and the Dakotas
12 North 12th St.
Minneapolis, Minnesota 55403

www.minndakjcrc.org

ISBN 978-0-9972633-0-5

Printed in the United States of America
1-41479-3000746-9/13/2016

The individuals whose stories appear in this book, who lived through the Holocaust and had the courage to open their wounds and chronicle their experiences, have our deepest gratitude. This book is dedicated to them and to their families.

Gary and Marsha Tankenoff

CONTENTS

HOLOCAUST SURVIVOR STORIES

AMERICAN LIBERATOR STORIES

THE POWER OF THE WITNESS
By DEBORAH E. LIPSTADT

The past decades have seen a proliferation of historical investigations, books, movies, and documentary studies of the Holocaust. Few if any areas of this terrible tragedy have not been probed by historians, philosophers, theologians, and social scientists. Without doubt there are still grave lacunae in this body of research, but to date a significant amount of material has been amassed. These works examine many different aspects of the Nazi destruction of the Jews including the complex role of the perpetrators, the experience of the victims, and the response of the Allies, the neutral nations, and agencies and religious bodies, notably the Vatican. The research draws on vast documentary archives, diaries, journals, newspapers, photographs, and even newsreels.

The most important and powerful historical source, yet one that is the most transitory, is that of the direct witnesses—the participants. Historians have long recognized the critical importance of the victims' personal accounts. Although documents and correspondence provide us with crucial information, the witnesses—and in this case, specifically the victims—speak with a particular moral force. They can speak in the first person: "This happened to me."

At the same time that we acknowledge the importance of their testimony we also recognize that their accounts are not foolproof. They may be limited by the vagaries of memory as well as by the fact that each victim witnessed "only" a small portion of this vast enterprise we call the Holocaust. Some lived in countries where Nazi rule was in place for an extended period of time prior to the beginning of the war, such as Germany, Austria, and portions of Czechoslovakia. Others were taken by surprise, as was the case in France, Poland, and the Soviet Union. Some individuals lived in ghettoes, while others were taken directly to camps. The situation in certain ghettoes differed radically from that in others. Life, and ultimately the way in which life was taken, differed from camp to camp. In certain instances survivors can only estimate dates, the duration of events, or the precise number of victims involved. Sometimes their memoirs may be influenced by ex post facto accounts of others. The ensuing years and the painful memories of their experiences have further made the act of remembering a difficult one.

For these reasons historians do not build the historical record solely on the recollections of the survivor. But despite these shortcomings of oral history, the memories recounted in this volume and the thousands of other interviews collected worldwide together constitute the "still, small" but most powerful voice that cries out in bitter testimony. These survivors felt the consequences of a world that went mad. They were there.

The voice of the witness has come to be important for yet another reason. Although denial seems impossible to imagine, some individuals attempt to deny that the Holocaust occurred. One is tempted to dismiss them as the historical equivalent of the "flat earth" theorists, but their claims have made some inroads. Certain anti-Semitic groups have enthusiastically embraced them. Others have used these claims for political and racial purposes. This small but industrious lot ignores the incredible number of facts that refute their "theory," including that the perpetrators did not deny their role. Echoing traditional anti-Semitic charges, they argue that the Holocaust is a great hoax perpetrated by the Jews on the entire world.

If only extreme anti-Semites accepted such ludicrous notions, there would be little room for concern. But some people—particularly those born after the Holocaust—seem willing to accept the validity of such arguments. Students and young people in this country, many of whom have a most hazy—at best—sense of history, are especially susceptible. The psychiatrist Walter Reich has observed that many young people seem willing to listen to these claims on the grounds that everything should be open to debate and that they can accept nothing as true if they do not personally see or experience it.

There are a variety of ways of responding to these specious claims, which deny the mountains of recorded fact. One tempting strategy is simply to ignore them. It is neither wise nor productive to enter into a debate with these so-called revisionists. To do so would grant them the validity they crave. Anyone subscribing to such outrageously false ideas is not likely to be bound by truth, so there is little to be gained by trying to engage him or her in normal intellectual interchanges. Moreover, for those who would try to deny the existence of the Holocaust, publicity is a lifeline. Without it they cannot make their voices heard, and their claims may well die a quick and merciful death.

There are, however, better ways of responding to these malicious charges. One is to educate potential listeners, to make it clear that the evidence of the Holocaust is so overwhelming that those who attempt to deny its existence are not really interested in pursuing truth but have other goals in mind. Facts may not deter the deniers, but they will demonstrate to others—particularly those born after the Holocaust—that these are not disinterested individuals engaged in a benign historical quest.

The other means of responding is to give the witnesses voice. Let those who were not there hear from those who were, who saw their families perish, who watched the trains bring thousands of unsuspecting individuals into the camps, who watched their parents and children be assigned by a Mengele or others like him to the wrong line, never to emerge from the buildings where they were sent to supposedly shower. No one individual can tell the whole story, but together the voices of those who survived have an unparalleled impact.

These witnesses' voices will be available to us for only a few more years. The youngest possible survivor of a concentration camp is now in his or her eighties. Soon there will be no one who will be able to say "I was there. This is what was done to me." That is the importance of this collection of voices. They are not ponderous. They are profound in their simplicity. They only seek to tell their individual stories and to convey their recollections of what happened to them and to their families. Many refrains repeat themselves, but one is most chilling. Over and over again survivors say, "I am the only one of my family who survived, all my relatives—parents, siblings, spouses, children, aunts, uncles, and cousins—were consumed by the fires of the Holocaust."

Another refrain is heard among the victims' voices: "I kept quiet for many years, but soon I will be gone and I must tell my children." It has taken many of the survivors a long time to be able to tell their stories. Many were convinced that the world was not interested, that once again, as had been the case while the Holocaust was in the making, their agony would be met with disbelief.

There is another set of voices in this collection: that of the liberators. Although the American army did not liberate the death camps in Poland, they witnessed the terrible brutality of camps such as Buchenwald,

Bergen-Belsen, and Dachau. The recollections of those who came upon these places before they had been sanitized and the survivors removed are critical because they were witness to the atrocities of the Third Reich. But they have value for yet another reason. They indicate how little those outside the whirlwind understood or were able to imagine what it was like. Only when they came face to face with the reality of the camps did they realize that the stories they'd heard were not exaggerations, that this truth could never be exaggerated.

Why had the world resisted this truth? The Holocaust unfolded slowly. Had the German people or the rest of the world wished to stop it in its early stages, they might well have succeeded. It is clear that the Nazis had tested the world to see how far they could go without encountering its wrath. In most instances the political and moral bodies of the world stood silently by. An important lesson is to be learned in the universal acquiescence to both the initial persecution and the ultimate horror. The one who stands silently by becomes a party to the crime. Standing mute in the face of evil is to cast one's vote on the side of the evil doer.

There is, however, an even more chilling lesson to be learned. The Germans did not conduct special tests in order to choose the most brutal and diabolical among them to participate in the annihilation of millions. The people who guarded the camps, ran the trains, delivered the supplies, gathered the Jews from their homes, and in a myriad of different ways made the Holocaust a reality were people who previously had led normal lives. An evil system and a diabolical leadership were able to elicit uncivilized behavior from a civilized people. The Holocaust was not committed by a cadre of sadistic beasts. Before the war—and in many cases after it—these people were doctors, lawyers, architects, teachers, clerks, farmers, and students. No apparent historical, social, cultural, or biological difference existed between these people and the rest of the world that would make such behavior predictable. This does not mean we are all capable of such atrocities. It does mean that it takes relatively little to turn "normal" humans into creatures capable of the most sadistic acts. This observation is not meant to suggest that it was simply the system that was at fault and the participants were guiltless. But until they crossed the dividing line between good and evil, they were relatively average, nondescript people.

Not all the perpetrators were beasts, not all the victims were heroes.

11

Many victims felt simply lucky to have survived, but in order to have survived they needed a unique strength and fortitude. Nor were all the liberators heroes. Some were simply soldiers whose paths led them to witness one of the great horrors of our times. Here too their voices teach us how the mundane can be transformed into the unfathomable, the everyday into the unimaginable.

Ultimately, the fundamental lesson of this collection is that if we let history and memory fade we risk letting such events happen again. The recollections collected here help form our defense against the repetition of history. The Hasidic teacher, the Ba'al Shem Tov, taught long ago that "in remembrance is the secret of redemption." The victims are not alone in their need of redemption. A world that allowed such crimes to happen and that continues to tolerate incredible evil in its midst is in continuous need of redemption. If we pay careful attention to these voices, they may lead one step closer in that direction.

Deborah E. Lipstadt, Ph.D. is the Dorot Professor of Modern Jewish History and Holocaust Studies at Emory University.

THE POWER OF TESTIMONY

More than 30 years ago, I was browsing among the sidewalk booksellers adjacent to Hyde Park in London. I found *The Black Book: The Nazi Crime Against the Jewish People* (Duell, Sloan and Pearce, New York, 1946). The book is a combination of indictment and historical narrative. It is a comprehensive—as much as was possible in 1946—telling of the story of the Holocaust. The book was written by representatives of the Jewish people: World Jewish Congress. (New York); Jewish anti-Fascist Committee (Moscow); Vaad Leeumi (National Council of the pre-state Jewish community of Mandatory Palestine); and the American Committee of Jewish Writers, Artists and Scientists (New York).

The *Black Book* was also dedicated to the preservation of historical memory of the *Shoah* in its rawest moment in the immediate aftermath of the war: "This is an obligation that we owe to the millions of Jewish martyrs who met a horrible death at the hands of the Nazis—we owe it to them that their death shall not be forgotten or go unpunished. We owe it to ourselves and our children to see that they shall not have died in vain." Indeed, 15 years later, prosecutor Gideon Hausner made survivor testimony the centerpiece of Israel's and humanity's case against Adolf Eichmann. The voices of the survivors and the voices of the perished were given life.

While hundreds of thousands of survivors were alive at the time of the Eichmann trial in Jerusalem, their numbers are a precious few a half-century later. They bore witness. They educated. They inspired. As Elie Wiesel noted at the dawn of the 21st century: "To listen to a survivor is to become a survivor." Now, in the words of eminent Holocaust historian Deborah Lipstadt, "the tyranny of biology" has taken its course.

Many years ago Laura Zelle recognized the importance of the stories of surviving the *Shoah* in her own family. She began videotaping the stories of her mother, aunt and uncle—Greek Jews who were among the very few survivors of the vicious German annihilation program in Greece. Righteous Gentiles saved the lives of Laura's family. She felt an imperative to tell the story.

The obligation to teach our children about the Holocaust to prevent the genocides of today and tomorrow has long been a JCRC priority. JCRC's Speakers Bureau of survivors has given, and continues to give, thousands of talks to tens of thousands of people throughout the Midwest. The original edition of this book—beautifully crafted by author and editor Rhoda Lewin under JCRC Executive Director Mort Ryweck in 1990—was an early attempt at telling the stories of Minnesota survivors and liberators. In addition to this new and updated edition of *Witnesses to the Holocaust*, JCRC has developed new approaches for telling survivor stories.

Laura's foresight in videotaping her family stories became the inspiration for the JCRC's Telly Award-winning *In the Shadow of the Acropolis*, the first of five half-hour documentaries about Minnesota Holocaust survivors. Four more documentaries were produced in conjunction with Minnesota survivor families: *But Some Survive, Esther's Story; I Was Given Life Twice, Hinda Kibort's Story; Sam Rafowitz, Remaking a Life*; and *Stolen Youth, David Fishel's Story*. The moving images of survivors became the basis of the JCRC traveling photo exhibit *Transfer of Memory*. Collaborating with photographer David Sherman, JCRC created a collection of beautiful photographic portraits and their accompanying life stories written by Lili Chester, herself a child of Holocaust survivors. *Transfer of Memory* has been seen by hundreds of thousands of people in the upper Midwest at universities, schools, synagogues, churches, historical societies and museums, resulting in much media coverage for its important mission. The exhibit hosts have developed supplemental programs teaching about the Holocaust, with the exhibit as the point of departure.

I remember many conversations with Holocaust survivor Fred Baron, z"l, about life in pre-war Vienna, surviving the *Shoah*, and life in post-war Minneapolis where he started anew with his wife, Judy, raised a family and started a successful business. We are grateful to all our survivors who have blessed us with their lives and the stories of their lives. A portrait of Fred and Judy is part of *Transfer of Memory*.

Transfer of Memory has led to additional creative programming. The St. Paul Chamber Orchestra is partnering with the JCRC for a series of concerts in 2016–2017 featuring the compositions of musicians who perished in the Holocaust or became emigres due to pre-war Nazi persecution. Additional thousands will have the opportunity to learn about the Holocaust in concert halls in St. Paul and Minneapolis, from the Ordway, to the University of Minnesota and area churches.

All these programs have ultimately led us back to a book. We are proud to introduce this new edition of *Witnesses to the Holocaust* to a new generation of readers. Text remains important as Jews are still "The People of the Book."

This 25th Anniversary edition of *Witnesses to the Holocaust* is the product of the vision and generosity of Gary and Marsha Tankenoff; the remarkable resources, skill and dedication of Joni Sussman and Harry Lerner at Lerner Publishing; the writing of Lili Chester; and the ongoing commitment of the JCRC to Holocaust education in the upper Midwest.

We also thank and acknowledge those with whom we work in partnership in Holocaust education and those whose support is critical to our mission of teaching about the Holocaust: Dr. Alejandro Baer of the University of Minnesota who follows in the footsteps of the late Professor Stephen Feinstein, z"l; Dr. Daniel Wildeson of St. Cloud State University; Dr. Rebecca Weaver-Hightower, Dr. Brian Urlacher, and Professor Gregory Gordon of the University of North Dakota; Dr. Andy Johnson of Bethel University; and all of the fifty schools, colleges, houses of worship, historical societies, community centers and museums which have hosted *Transfer of Memory*. (We note also, with sadness, the passing of St. Cloud State President Earl H. Potter III who was a great champion of Holocaust education on his campus.)

We also are deeply grateful for the support for Holocaust education from the Minneapolis Jewish Federation and the Jewish Federation of Greater St. Paul and the support of the following foundations: Tankenoff Families Foundation; Sheldon and Lili Chester Philanthropic Fund; Oren and Sharron Steinfeldt Family Fund; Beverly Foundation of Minnesota; Otto Bremer Foundation of Minnesota; Kelen Family Foundation; and Allianz of America with particular thanks to Peter Lefkin and Rev. Christopher Worthley of the Allianz Foundation.

Steve Hunegs
Executive Director
Jewish Community Relations Council of Minnesota and the Dakotas

THE AFTERMATH OF THE HOLOCAUST

Every Holocaust survivor you'll meet in this book has a unique story to tell, often brutal but always demonstrating an emotional and inspiring spirit of survival. Some people were survivors of horrific concentration camp experiences. Others survived in hiding or fighting with partisans. It may not always seem so as you read these stories, but these individuals were the lucky ones, the ones who survived.

The liberators of the concentration camps, some of whose experiences appear in this book, also have remarkable stories. In 1945, when Allied troops entered the concentration camps, they discovered the remains of hundreds of thousands of Holocaust victims. But they also found concentration camp survivors, many barely alive, most suffering from starvation and disease.

After liberation, many Jews were afraid to return to their former homes because of the anti-Semitism that persisted in parts of Europe even after the war. With few possibilities for places to go, many Holocaust survivors were initially housed in refugee centers and displaced persons camps set up by the Allied armies. There, survivors were able to receive medical care, shelter, food and clothing, as well as to begin their searches for surviving family members, and to make plans for what their post-war lives would be.

Social service agencies, such as the American Jewish Joint Distribution Committee, provided Holocaust survivors with food and clothing, while the Red Cross tried to help reunite survivors with family members.

But survivors had few immigration options right after the war. The United States and other Allies had restrictions on the number of refugees they would take, and the State of Israel (then Palestine) was still under British rule. But in 1945 and again in 1948, President Harry Truman loosened quota restrictions for Immigration to the U.S. for those displaced by the Nazis, and with the establishment of the State of Israel in May 1948, Jewish refugees were able to begin coming to the United States and to Israel.

Many immigrants entered the U.S. through Ellis Island in New York and then ventured on to other states based on where local sponsorship for them was available. For Minnesotans, the Joint Distribution Center, the Jewish Family Service of St. Paul, and the Jewish Family and Children's Service of Minneapolis helped survivor families relocate, find housing, seek work, and connect with the local Jewish community.

Re-establishing a life was also not simple. As a descendent of a Greek child survivor, I have inherited a particular legacy rooted in lost family, lost traditions, lost homeland, and lost heritage. I have watched my mother try to rebuild her life and connections and learn how difficult and emotionally draining it can be. I have documented her family's story and understand the power of the words from the eminent historian Simon Dubnov, who over and over implored his Riga ghetto: *"Yidden, schreibt un farschreibt"*—"Jews, write it all down."

For me, the Holocaust has always been intensely personal. It may have ended over two decades before I was born, but I have always understood that my mother and her family were victims of a worldwide annihilation of a people affecting future generations for years to come. It took my family decades to learn the circumstances leading to our family member's deaths or survival. The details that surround our story and breathe life into our history were passed down through oral storytelling.

Rhoda Lewin, the editor of the first edition of this book, wrote that there were no guarantees for survival in Hitler's Europe, especially for Jews. "A carpenter or a mechanic had a better chance than a shopkeeper. It helped to be young and physically fit, and sometimes to have blond hair and blue eyes, or to have money or jewelry with which to buy forged papers, black market food, or the route to freedom. Luck was often the most important factor, and the luckiest ones left Europe before or during the war.

"Many Holocaust survivors did not even tell their own children what had happened to them, why there was a number tattooed on their arm, or why the children had no grandparents, no aunts and uncles, no cousins. Some could not, or did not want to, tell their children what cruelties human beings could commit, what they had suffered, or what they had to do in order to survive. Others remained silent because they could not answer their own questions: How could human beings treat their fellow human beings with such cruelty? Why was I chosen to survive? Moreover, they were silenced by well-meaning people who did not want to listen, who said, 'It's over, and we must put the past behind. Forget those terrible things, begin a new life.'"

Then, in the mid-1970s, historians and survivors began to realize that the Holocaust story had not been told and that the survivors would not be around to bear witness for future generations. Elie Wiesel and Primo Levi began to write their stories and it would take decades more for hundreds of thousands of survivor testimonies to be collected by Steven Spielberg's Shoah Visual History Foundation as part of the USC Shoah Foundation archives. Through these foundational efforts, a platform of first person testimony began to emerge as a vital piece in Holocaust education. Using these pieces of collected testimony, the JCRC created a Minnesota Holocaust Survivor educational film series showcasing the stories of the Ackos, Latarus, Kibort, Rafowitz and Fishel families.

Through a dedicated Minnesota Holocaust Survivors Speakers Bureau, hundreds of thousands of people across the state have heard eye-witness testimony from Jews who were meant for annihilation. Second generation, third generations and now fourth generation family members are beginning to retell stories of survival and continue to illustrate what intolerance and hatred against a people can look like in a civilized society.

The stories in this book will live on and are now in your hands. They are for you to read, learn from, and continue to retell. It is inevitable that the enormity of the Holocaust will recede in public awareness but the stories on these pages is how we tell the story of the Holocaust—not as a single monolithic event, but as the story of six million individuals, murdered one by one.

In the words of Sara Bloomfield, Director of the United States Holocaust Memorial Museum, "We are in the midst of a transition to a world without eyewitnesses. And we are losing our survivors, our very best teachers. We are going to have ever greater challenges to bring this history to our children who will have had no exposure to Holocaust survivors and more exposure to hate and denial on the internet. Everything that the Nazis tried to destroy, we are trying to save. We're in a race against time to collect stories and retell them. When the survivors and all the eyewitnesses are gone, these stories will be the sole authentic witness to the Holocaust."

In this book, we are capturing eye-witness testimonies and making them accessible to you. This is the power to teach and inspire the next generation as we enter a world without eye-witnesses.

This 25th Anniversary Edition of *Witnesses to the Holocaust* is dedicated to the families of the book's Second Generation writers and editors: the Ackos family, the Kibort family and the Latarus family.

Laura Zelle,
Director, Tolerance Minnesota and Holocaust Education
Jewish Community Relations Council of Minnesota and the Dakotas

"It happened but it could have been prevented."
—Elie Wiesel.

ACKNOWLEDGMENTS

There were no records showing how many Holocaust survivors or liberators lived in Minnesota. Social service agencies that assisted survivors when they arrived in the United States did not keep records. In 1990, under the leadership of Mort Ryweck and Carol Wirtschafter, the Jewish Community Relations Council of Minnesota and the Dakotas worked with Rhoda Lewin to interview, solicit funding, and write the original book, *Witnesses to the Holocaust*. We thank Mort, Carol and Rhoda for their foresight in creating the original book.

Thank you to Marsha and Gary Tankenoff for their financial support in producing this 25th Anniversary edition.

Thank you to contributing writers Steve Hunegs and Lili Chester. Thank you to Joni Sussman at Lerner Publishing for all her editing guidance and continued dedication to Holocaust education. Thank you to David Sherman for his beautiful portraits of local Holocaust survivors that appear in this book.

This 25th Anniversary edition honors the memory of the Minnesota community of Holocaust survivors who built Holocaust programming and education through their courage to retell their stories over the past six decades. This book is a snapshot of some of those stories and we regret that not every story could be included.

Thank you to the University of Minnesota Center for Holocaust and Genocide Studies, Dr. Alejandro Baer, Demetrios Vital, and Jennifer Hammer for your permission to include the archival information housed at the center. Posthumously we thank Dr. Stephen Feinstein, who established the strong foundation on which all Minnesota Holocaust educators stand today. His gifts live on through subsequent work from the primary resources housed at the Center.

Author and historian Rhoda G. Lewin, Ph.D. brought this oral history book to life 25 years ago. Rhoda's long-standing career in newspaper reporting, publication editing, public relations, and teaching journalism at the University of Wisconsin/Superior and the University of Minnesota was a gift to our community. She wrote a monthly column for the American Jewish World for ten years and was a founding member of the Minnesota Independent Scholars Forum and the Jewish Historical Society of the Upper Midwest. Rhoda was the author of two books, *Witnesses to the Holocaust: An Oral History* and *Images of America: Jewish Community of North Minneapolis*.

THE SURVIVORS

Many people have come to use *concentration camp* as a generic term to describe the places where the Germans imprisoned or exterminated Jews before and during World War II. Actually, there were many kinds of camps, and many kinds of prisoners. There were slave labor camps in ghettoes and other locations, where Jews and non-Jews from countries occupied by the Germans worked in factories, quarried stone, built roads and anti-tank ditches, and performed other work for their German captors. There were prison camps intended at first for the Nazis' political opponents and, later, for prisoners of war. And there were the extermination camps, where millions, almost all of them Jews, were systematically put to death.

Death came in many forms. Men, women, and children of all ages were gassed, burned alive, starved to death. They died of typhus, tuberculosis, or other diseases. Or they were murdered in other ways by sadistic guards or by doctors performing medical experiments.

Some Jews survived the Holocaust because they were hidden by non-Jews, who risked their own lives to save friends, or, sometimes, by total strangers. Some fought with the partisans or the Resistance. Some hid in cellars or closets or forest bunkers, sometimes for years. Some escaped to other countries. Some had skills the Germans needed for the war effort and were assigned to labor camps or factory work. And some passed as non-Jews.

Examples of many of these kinds of survivor stories are included in this book.

SAM ACKOS, MARY ACKOS CALOF AND EVELYN ACKOS ETTINGER

ATHENS, GREECE

"The greatest author of the world can never describe the truth of this Holocaust. There is no pen sharp enough to write exactly what happened, no mind big enough to believe the things that took place."

Sam Ackos was only twelve when his father was taken away by the Germans in 1944, and he became the head of his family, shining Nazis' shoes and trading on the black market for food for his mother and four little sisters.

"My father was a wheeler dealer guy," said Sam. "He'd go to a warehouse and buy blankets, put them on his shoulder or pushcart, and go to the neighborhoods to sell to the ladies. Also he was a goldsmith—buying and selling, gold and copper and silver.

"We respected and loved God. I attended synagogue on all the High Holidays, to keep our customs alive. But gentiles were our friends, classmates, neighbors. Religion had not much to do in the neighborhood except at Passover, when it was also Easter and Good Friday. Greek mothers would frighten little Greek boys and girls saying that if they weren't good, they would be given to the Jews, and we would prick them with pins to take their blood for the Passover matzah!

"October 28, 1940, the Italians attacked Greece. Everybody went to fight for the freedom of our country, and Mussolini had to ask Hitler for help. In April the Nazis marched into Greece, and everything turned upside down. The last thing Greek radio said was, 'Everybody has to fight against the Nazis, even if it costs his life. Long live Greece!'

"In two months, everything had disappeared from Greece. Our father had saved gold and we were selling on the black market to buy food. One pound of beans and three pounds of bread would last the six of us three days.

We lost more people from starvation than we lost from bullets.

"There wasn't such a thing as a ghetto or forced labor in Greece. There was no wearing of yellow stars. Anybody over fifteen had to have an I.D. but in every neighborhood one or two Greeks would risk their own lives to give the Jews false I.D.s, claiming the Jew was Greek Orthodox.

"We hid radios inside wells, and in the afternoon we would get them out to listen to the London BBC. The penalty for listening to the BBC was death.

"We heard Winston Churchill say, 'Greek people, if you damage one screw out of the great German machine, you lead us one step toward victory.' Kids were doing everything and anything to damage the conquerors. We stole fuel, blew tires, did sabotage.

"My mother's sister had a non-Jewish friend, a very well-to-do lady who had a house in a suburb of Athens. In '43, when we heard the Jews of Salonika were put in concentration camps, my father went with the partisans and we hid in that lady's house, in a small basement room. Then my father came home, and we came back to our house.

"Toward 1944 the great Nazi snake was dying. The Nazi general in charge of Athens promised through the archbishop that he would not harm the Jewish people if every Saturday the men would present themselves in the synagogue for an hour. For several weeks the Jews were mustering at the synagogue, but March 25, 1944, was a tragic story.

"I was helping my family by selling cigarettes on the black market, and one place I could do a little business. was at the gathering of the Greek Jews in the synagogue. That Saturday the doors of the synagogue suddenly closed, with all the heads of the Jewish families inside. A German gave me a good kick, and said, 'Get out!' I ran home and told what happened. My mother's two brothers were at the synagogue, and one brother's wife and her two kids wanted to go with her husband. Mother's idea was to take us all and follow her husband, too, but I objected strongly.

"They put the Jews in trucks and took them outside Athens to a small concentration camp. Then word spread that the Nazis took the records of the synagogue, so they knew where every Jewish house was located, and they were confiscating whatever they could and wanted to take everybody to the camp. So again we walked the ten miles to our gentile friend for shelter.

"I was shining Nazis' shoes in Constitution Square in exchange for a little food. My mother and I were also wheeling and dealing on the black market, with small gold coins my father made during the good days. To buy food you had to go way out to the small villages. Ten miles, fifteen miles, the farther you went, the more likely the Nazis would not find you. Farmers were afraid to come to Athens, but they were willing to sell for gold.

"After the war, we heard they kept the Jews in the camp for a couple of days and then loaded them onto trains to Auschwitz, Buchenwald, Dachau. According to survivors from Auschwitz, my father was part of the plot to blow up the crematoriums. One person said they saw him selected to the right for work, another said they saw him selected to the left for the gas chambers. We didn't know what was true and not true, but he did not come home. Father was very strong, very brave. Mother thought Nazi bullets would not be strong enough to kill him.

"The day the war ended, the Nazi flag came down from the Acropolis, and the Greek flag went up. The radios were playing patriotic songs and everybody had such joy. Then our home was confiscated by a Nazi collaborator, but we could not prove he was a collaborator, so from four rooms we ended up with only one, and were forced to be neighbors to the collaborator.

"My dad owned a taxicab, which was very unique at that time. The Nazis were confiscating anything with wheels, so my father took the cab apart. To make a living after the war, my mother and I took the parts of the cab out and put it back together.

"Israel was reborn at that time, and Greece was one of the main links to Israel by sea. But a gentleman who knew father praised America so much, and said that in America my four sisters would not need a dowry to get husbands, so my mother knew that the only place in the world her kids could be happy was America.

"We sold our taxicab to pay part of the transportation, and the Joint Distribution Committee paid the rest. We could stay in New York and live like Greeks, like living in our old neighborhood in a different part of the world, but mother didn't want that. We came to Minnesota to live like Americans.

Sam Ackos has four younger sisters. When the war ended, Evelyn was eight and Mary was six. Their memories are of hunger, hiding, and pretending to be Christians; a tall, loving father who disappeared; and life in an orphanage after the war.

"When we went into hiding, we put all our belongings in storage with neighbors," said Mary Calof, "and when we came back they wouldn't give them back to us. My mother told us the court said, 'Why do you Jews make trouble? They should've killed you all.' So I always had a very strong feeling of being scared that people knew I was Jewish, even after the war.

"My mother's emotional state, on finding out she was alone, left with five children, was very difficult. There was an orphanage that was supposed to give parents the chance to put their homes and lives together, so my mother put her two youngest, Evelyn and me, in the orphanage. My mother used to come to visit, loaded down with food like raw eggs, and I would cry when she left. I was there two years, until they disbanded it.

"I was twelve when we came to America, and the community sent us to camp. My mother never worked during her marriage, but here she worked as a seamstress. She never complained, but she never really made the transition to America. She was forever looking toward Greece."

"After I became a U.S. citizen, I went back to Greece to visit," said Evelyn Ackos Ettinger. "The pull back to my native land remains as strong today. My father was a go-getter. He had a jewelry stand in the square in Athens, and I remember going into my mother's room and seeing on top of the dresser a stack of money. So even with the Germans there, we had food—potatoes, wheat. Dad was sharing it with people across the street who had no food.

"I was seven when my father was taken. Word had gotten out that something terrible was taking place at the synagogue. My mother went to the synagogue, but my dad made her go back and told her to take us to this friend, a Christian woman of very aristocratic background. She put her life on the line to save us.

"In that area there were many Jewish families being hidden, even though we were just two blocks away from a German camp. Nothing was really normal, so people could accept that we were relatives from a northern village. But I had to go to church with my mother and pretend to cross myself. After the war, mother would not celebrate any Jewish holidays. She refused. We used to go to the synagogue without her."

MANFRED (FRED) AMRAM

HANNOVER, GERMANY

"I was six years old the next time the men in uniform returned with their terrifying knock. I, the man of the house, went to the door, unlocked it and sprang out of the way as it was pushed open."

Fred Amram was a small boy of five when he first encountered the Nazis. He describes his first encounter with the Nazis, from his memoir **We're In America Now: A Survivor's Stories (Holy Cow! Press, 2016),** *from which this story is taken.*

"In 1938 I was five years old and I could already feel my childhood slipping away," remembers Fred Amram. "One day a loud demanding knock frightened Mutti (mother). An even louder, more insistent knock caused Mutti to jump. She sprang to the door, inhaled and turned the doorknob. The push from the other side knocked her to the floor. 'I want Meinhardt Amram,' demanded the handsome man. To me, he looked like a uniformed giant. 'Gestapo,' announced the officer in his intimidating black uniform and calf-high leather boots. His visor cap displayed an eagle and a death mask—or was it a skull?

"'Meinhardt Amram is my husband.' Mutti responded. 'I want him at once,' demanded the officer. 'He's out on business,' Mutti said almost belligerently. 'Have him report to Gestapo headquarters as soon as he returns.' He clicked his heels, gave an almost imperceptible bow, raised his right arm to a 45-degree angle, and with a 'Heil Hitler' he was gone. In 1938 such unwanted visits were not unusual at the homes of Jews living in Hannover, Germany. Even before Kristallnacht—Crystal Night, the Night of Broken Glass—Jewish men disappeared. Later, the Gestapo came for the families. But in the early days they came only for the men.

"Papa wasn't home. The truth I learned much later was that he had 'ways of knowing.' We lived on the fourth floor of a five-story apartment building. He would disappear 'downstairs.' I never found out how far 'downstairs' he went, to the apartment of righteous Christians who found a hiding place for him. When he returned, I told Papa about the black uniform and the death mask and the red armband and the gun. My Papa did not report to the Gestapo. 'They'll be back,' he announced with certainty.

"One day we heard the insistent knock. No matter which officer came, the knock was always the same. This time three officers entered, all in shiny boots and all carrying drawn pistols. One officer told my mother and me to stand in

Manfred (Fred) Amram

the corner, pointing with his gun to the preferred spot. The two holstered their guns and started searching. I held tight to Mutti's skirt.

"'Radios. Where are your radios?' Mutti explained that we owned only one. 'It's in the living room.' The truth wasn't enough. The gangsters emptied every wardrobe and every cabinet. When the search was over, our guard announced, 'Jews will not listen to radios. Never! We will check.' As if it were rehearsed, the three thieves gave us a 'Heil Hitler' in perfect unison, and they were gone with our radio. At supper, Mutti told Papa that we should all go into hiding. 'They will kill you. They will kill our son.' Papa, ever hopeful, gave his usual biblical assurance. 'This too shall pass. ' Mutti wasn't assured. They argued past my bedtime.

"Knock! Knock! Knock! Always that triple knock. 'Meinhardt Amram.' Mutti's response never wavered. 'Meinhardt Amram is my husband and he is out on business. 'Mommy explained that he drove around suburban

Hannover where he sold fabric by the yard to housewives who made clothing for themselves and their families. Mutti's glance fell on a closed door near the entryway. The S.S. officer saw the glance and a search ensued. With a pistol drawn, another officer entered our apartment and opened the door to my favorite room in the apartment, Papa's storage room. Perfectly white walls with perfectly white shelves showed off bolts of fabric in every imaginable color and texture. Sometimes Papa let me stand on his ladder so that I could feel the different textures: wool and silk, cotton and linen. I loved Papa's fabric room better than going to the park, even better than eating ice cream. The colors made my heart beat faster.

"Finding the cloth, the two officers talked quietly, both with their guns drawn and aimed at Mutti and me. Even as a five-year, I had seen the police and civilians smash Jewish shop windows. Looting Jewish stores was by now common. Jewish shopkeepers were beaten, humiliated and then hauled away. The uniformed officers returned with three additional men and hauled away every last bolt of fabric.

"That night, Papa didn't come home until well after supper. He was dirty and tired. Papa explained that the S.S. had traced him through his automobile license plates. They arrested him, confiscated his car and brought him to a construction site. There he worked with other Jewish slave laborers under the supervision of armed guards. Papa described how workers at the site had been shot because they fainted from the hot sun and heavy work. Papa now had no income and would be forced to work as a slave seven days each week. He returned home after my bedtime and he left before I awoke. I had no Papa.

"I was six years old the next time the men in uniform returned with their terrifying knock. I, the man of the house, went to the door, unlocked it and sprang out of the way as it was pushed open. They had come to search. This time I stood in front of my mother—not behind. I looked straight at the lead officer with my arms crossed. I guessed that was the proper posture for a grown-up. I never regained my childhood."

Reprinted with permission from essay by Fred Amram

SAM BANKHALTER

LODZ, POLAND

"In Auschwitz I had to pick up people with typhus, still living, take them to the gas chambers, then to the crematorium. You don't think, you just try to survive. I was fourteen years old."

Sam Bankhalter's father was a manufacturer of prefabricated wooden houses, a Hebrew scholar, and an ardent Zionist who helped young Poles who wanted to go to Palestine. Sam was running an errand for his father when the Nazis caught him and sent him to Auschwitz.

"There had always been anti-Semitism in Poland," said Sam. "'The slogan, even before Hitler was 'Jew, get out of here and go to Palestine.' As Hitler came to power, there was not a day at school I was not spit on or beaten up.

"I was at summer camp when the Germans invaded Poland. The camp directors told us to find our own way home. We walked many miles with airplanes over our heads, dead people in the streets. At home there were blackouts. I was just a kid, tickled when I was issued a flashlight and a gas mask. The Polish army was equipped with horse-and-buggies, the Germans were all on trucks and tanks.

"The German occupation was humiliation from Day 1. If Jewish men had a beard and side curls, the Germans cut the beard, cut the side curls, laughed at you, beat you up a little bit. Then the Germans took part of Lodz, put barbed wire around it, and all the Jews had to assemble in this ghetto area. You had to leave in five or ten minutes or half an hour, so you couldn't take much with you.

"The Jewish community chose my father to run the cemetery, to organize burials and clean up the streets. They brought in frozen Jewish soldiers, hundreds and hundreds. I helped bury them.

"We were the first ones in Auschwitz. We built it. What you got for clothing was striped pants and the striped jacket, no underwear, no socks.

In wintertime we put paper in our shoes, and we used to take empty cement sacks and put a string in the top, put two together, and wear one in back and one in front to keep warm.

"If they told us to do something, we went to do it. There was no yes or no, no choices. I worked in the crematorium for about eleven months. I saw Dr. Mengele's experiments on children, Later, in Buchenwald, I saw Ilse Koch with a hose, trying to get pressure to make a hole in a woman's stomach. I saw them cutting Greek people. I was in Flossenburg for two weeks, where they shot 25,000 Russian soldiers, and we had to burn the bodies. Every day the killings, the hangings, the shootings, the crematorium smell, the ovens, and the smoke going out the chimney.

"I knew everybody, knew every trick to survive. I was one of the youngest in Auschwitz, and I was 'adopted' by a lot of the older people, especially the fathers. Whole families came into Auschwitz together, and there was Dr. Mengele, who was saying 'right, left, left, right,' and you knew, right there, who was going to the gas chamber and who was not. Most of the men broke down when they knew their wives and their children —three-, five-, nine-year-olds—went to the gas chambers. In fact, one of my brothers committed suicide in Auschwitz because he couldn't live with knowing his wife and children were dead.

"I was able to see my family when they came into Auschwitz in 1944. I had a sister. She had a little boy a year old. Everybody that carried a child went automatically to the gas chamber, so my mother took the child. My sister survived, but she always suffered, feeling she was a part of killing my mother.

"I waved to my mother and I went over to my father and said, 'Dad, where is God? They even kill rabbis! What has happened?' His only answer to me was, 'This is the way God wants it.' This was the last time I spoke to my father.

"The Germans liquidated Auschwitz a few months before liberation. They put us in railroad boxcars, 125 men in each car, hundreds of cars. We couldn't sit, we couldn't stand, we couldn't lie down. We were sealed in. No food, nothing. It was January, and I was so thirsty I licked the frost off the metal, even when my tongue got stuck and pieces ripped off.

We wound up in Buchenwald. But when the guards tried to take us out of Buchenwald, I wouldn't go. I could barely walk, and I knew I wouldn't make it. There's another fellow alive today in Germany, and one in Israel, because the three of us crawled into a septic hole under the barracks and hid.

"For three days I was in that hole, listening to the guns, closer and closer. Then I passed out. I guess. it was American soldiers who dragged me out of the hole and flew me to Marseille, to a hospital. After I recuperated I went all over Europe, looking for people. I was nineteen years old, and I had nobody. I couldn't even remember my grandparents' names, so I could look for them. Then one night in a dream the name came to me. This is the way I found my aunt, who lives now in Paris. You start to put your life together. I was living in a displaced persons camp for a while, then I went out on my own in Frankfurt. I worked for the American military as an interpreter. I picked people up in Poland, smuggling them to Palestine, smuggling food, clothing. I sent people from Hamburg to Haifa, but the British sent them back. I got married, and my wife was working with me.

"In 1949 we settled in Israel. Israel was a brand new country. I worked smuggling ammunition, got into buying mechanical equipment for kibbutzim, and built one of the biggest irrigation plants in the world. I had a job that took me all over the world—Burma, Africa.

"As a Jew, I don't think you can feel as good anywhere as you can feel in Israel. But there were terrorists all the time. We were coming home from a birthday party and were ambushed with machine guns shooting at us, killing three people. My daughter, ten years old, was terrified, couldn't sleep at night, couldn't concentrate in school. The doctor said, 'You have to get away from this atmosphere.' I wanted to stay in Israel, but we came to the United States in 1956.

"Once you start fighting for your life, all the ethics are gone. You live by circumstances. There is no pity. You physically draw down to the point where you cannot think anymore, where the only thing is survival, and maybe a little hope that if I survive, I'm going to be with my grandchildren and tell them this story.

"In the camps, death actually became a luxury. We used to say, 'Look at how lucky he is. He doesn't have to suffer anymore.' I was a lucky guy. I survived, and I felt pretty good about it. But then I felt guilty living! My children—our friends were their 'aunts' and 'uncles.' They didn't have a grandfather, a grandmother, a cousin, a holiday as a family.

"As you grow older, you think about it, certain faces come back to you. You remember your home, your brothers, children that went to the crematorium. You wonder, how did your mother and father feel when they were in the gas chamber? Many nights I hear voices screaming in those first few minutes in the gas chamber, and I don't sleep.

"But how quickly the world forgets."

FRED BARON

VIENNA, AUSTRIA

"I was liberated in Bergen-Belsen. I remember clutching a can of condensed milk in my hand. I sat in the mud among the dead, and I found a rusty nail and tried to punch a hole in the can. Then I took a pebble, but the pebble was to me like a rock. I didn't even have the strength to open a can of milk."

Fred Baron was fifteen when the Germans marched into Vienna in 1938. His parents were well-to-do, assimilated Jews; both died in the Holocaust.

"I had a wonderful youth," said Fred. "I went to concerts, to the opera, my parents sent us to camp in the summertime. But in Europe even small children were aware that life is not always peaceful. The first thing we learned in school was military history —the wars and rebellions and constant occupations.

"My father was really an agnostic and my mother was not observant anymore, and my Jewish education came once a week in the public schools, the same as Catholics and Protestants. We were born in Austria and spoke German and felt and looked just like anybody else.

"In March 1938 the Germans marched into Austria. What had evolved in Germany over five years happened in Austria within a matter of weeks.

"One of my best friends became overnight an outspoken Austrian Nationalist and an anti-Semite. I was kicked out of high school. My father's store was closed down. Bank accounts were closed, people lost their jobs. Jews were not allowed to practice as professionals. We were penniless, forced to share our apartment with other Jews. Jews could not go to any public building or any parks. We could not go to a library or movie. We were not allowed to ride on public transportation except under certain conditions, and then only on the rear platform. We could not go into a store, except one hour a day. Even if we had money we were not allowed to buy many things, including certain foods, because they were just not sold to Jews. I went to a soup kitchen every day to bring home our only meal.

"On Kristallnacht I went downstairs to see whether it was safe to go out, and a lieutenant spotted my yellow badge and took me to a makeshift jail. My mother found me after a few hours. She had relatives in Hungary, and she managed to free me by waving some kind of Hungarian document in the Nazis' faces.

"My father had friends in England, and they were all trying to help us get out, but like America and every other country, England made tremendous difficulties for Jews to immigrate. The only exception was for a few Jewish children. These friends made it possible for my sister to join one of the children's transports early in 1939. My parents felt very sad about sending their twelve-year-old daughter away to a strange country, to live with a strange family in a small town.

"On September 1, 1939, war broke out with Poland, and after a few weeks they took Jewish people on trains and dumped them in ghettoes in Polish cities. Many of our friends were taken this way. My father saw his family, everything, going down the drain. He became very sick, and there was no medical treatment for Jews, so he didn't get any treatment and soon died.

"My mother and I were hiding one night here and one night there, with non-Jewish friends. Anybody hiding a Jew was subject to terrible penalties, so to ask even a close friend to hide you was not an easy thing to do. We also tried to hide in Jewish apartments where the people had already been deported.

"I found work at the railroad station and was given security for myself and my mother. I worked carrying pig-iron on my shoulders. In fall of 1941, the German extermination policy really got running. Transports to the east were increasing, so my mother and I went over the border at night to Hungary.

Fred Baron (center) recuperating
in Swedish hospital

"In Hungary I tried to get legal documentation so we could get food stamps. I traveled to a little town where somebody with connections was supposedly able to give us the necessary papers. But a crime had been committed in the town, and as soon as they saw me, a stranger, they put me in jail. The judge said I was innocent but wanted to send me back to Austria! I tried to explain that being sent back there was like a death sentence, and finally the judge dismissed me because I had some papers from my father, who had been an officer in the Austro-Hungarian army in the first World War. I was given papers that I was a legal resident of Hungary and could get food tickets.

"In December 1941, the Hungarian authorities got hold of my mother and put her in jail in Budapest. Because we entered the country without papers they told her they would deport her unless I joined her in jail.

"We were sent to an internment camp in northeastern Hungary. There were separate buildings for men and women, but I saw my mother from time to time. Later all the male Jews were sent to a prison camp near the Slovakian border, and my mother was freed to live with relatives in Hungary. She sent me letters, a package containing some clothing, even a cake. When the German S.S. completed the occupation of Hungary in the spring of 1944, my mother again was put into a camp, and that was the last I heard from her.

"I was marched with the local Jewish population —men, women, and children —eight or ten hours, to a small railroad station. Nobody told us where we were going. We were forced into railroad cars, 100 to 120 in one car, like sardines, without food, without water, without any sanitary facility.

34

The cars were sealed and we stood there for maybe half a day before even moving. Finally, began the slow trip to nowhere. There were children in our car, and old people. People got sick, died, and some went insane. It was an absolute, indescribable hell. I really don't know how many days and nights we were in that living hell on wheels. When we finally stopped, they tore open the railroad cars and we were blinded by light, because our eyes were just not used to light anymore. We saw funny-looking characters wearing striped pajama-like uniforms with matching caps, with great big sticks in their hands. They were screaming and yelling in all languages to jump out of the cars. I didn't know where I was. All around us were barracks and barbed wire and machine gun towers, and in the distance I saw what looked like a huge factory with black smoke coming out of chimneys. I noticed a peculiar smell in the air and also a fine dust, subduing the light. The sunshine was not bright but there were birds singing. It was a beautiful day.

"We were marched through a meadow filled with yellow flowers and one of the fellows next to me just turned and walked straight into the meadow. The guards cried out to him to stop, but he didn't hear or he didn't want to. He just kept slowly marching into the meadow, and then they opened up with machine guns and the man fell down dead. And that was my reception to Auschwitz.

"We were separated, men and women, and formed rows of fives. I found myself in front of a very elegantly dressed German officer. He was wearing boots and white gloves and he carried a riding whip, and with the whip he was pointing left or right, left or right. Whichever direction he pointed, guards pushed the person in front of him either left or right. I was twenty-one years old and in pretty good shape, but older people were sent to the other side and marched away.

"We had to undress and throw away all belongings except our shoes. We were chased through a cold shower, and we stood shivering in the night air until we were told to march to a barracks. We were handed prisoner uniforms—a jacket, pants, and a sort of beanie and a metal dish. We didn't really know what had happened yet. We were absolutely numb. A non-Jewish kapo, an Austrian with a hard, weather-beaten face, told us, 'You have arrived at hell on earth.' He had been in prison since 1938, and he gave us basic concepts on how to stay alive.

"'Don't trust anybody,' he said. 'Don't trust your best friend. Look out for yourself. Be selfish to the point of obscenity. Try and stay alive from one minute to the next. Don't let down for one second. Always try and find out where the nearest guards are and what they are doing. Don't volunteer for anything. And don't get sick, or you will be a goner in no time.'

"Auschwitz was gigantic—rows and rows of barracks as far as the eye could see, subdivided by double strings of electric barbed wire. There were Hungarian and Polish Jews and a great number of Greeks, many Dutch Jews, some French, Germans.

"Food was our main interest in life. In the morning we received what they called coffee—black water. We worked until noon, then we got a bowl of soup. In the evening we received another bowl of vegetable soup, a little piece of bread, and sometimes a tiny little piece of margarine or sugar or some kind of sausage. And that was the food for the day.

"Suicides happened all the time, usually by hanging, at night. One fellow threw himself in front of a truck. It just broke his arm, but the S.S. guards beat him to a pulp, and in the morning he was dead. A tremendous number of transports were coming in. The gas chambers could not keep up, so they were burning people in huge pits. Some of the smaller children were thrown in alive. We could hear the screams day and night, but sometimes the human mind can take just so much and then it just closes up and refuses to accept what is happening just 100 feet away.

"I was sent to Silesia, to a small town belonging to the Grossrosen administrative area. The Germans built bunks in an empty factory, encircled the area with barbed wire, built machine gun towers, and—presto!—a slave labor camp for a thousand people. We were working right in small German towns, widening the roads and making them stronger so the Germans could bring in heavy equipment against the Russians. I don't like to have anybody tell me the German people did not know what was going on because I could see hundreds of them every day and they could see us. We couldn't be mistaken for anything but prisoners! We were walking skeletons, we had our hair shorn, we had these blue and white striped uniforms. And we were guarded by heavily armed S.S. as if we would be the most precious possession the world would have to offer.

"When their wives and families came to see them, our guards were concerned husbands, normal human beings. But when it came to the prisoners, they were absolute animals, and they became more and more vicious as they saw their own end nearing. Toward the very end, when these dregs of humanity were sent to war, the Germans brought in old people or severely wounded soldiers as guards, and these showed us much more humanity.

"In December 1944, we could hear the rumbling of the approaching Russian armies and guns firing. We saw German refugees, civilians, coming from the east and going west. And pretty soon we saw them going east from the west. Germany was being compressed, and they were running from the Russian and American armies.

"In February we were marched on foot to Czechoslovakia, over the mountains. It was cold, snowing. Everybody who lagged behind was shot, so we learned to sleep while walking, to urinate while walking. Then we were put in open railroad cars, without provisions, freezing. A sympathetic German in charge of this train kept us alive by giving us hot water from the engine.

"They took us to Bergen-Belsen, a nightmare of a different sort. It was crowded, there was hardly any food, water was nonexistent. But we were not hounded by guards or worked to death. We starved to death. At first people who died were put in mass graves. It took four of us to drag one body to the graves, four dying people dragging one dead one. Then there were so many, they were stacked like cord wood at every corner of the barracks. Mountains appeared, mountains of bodies.

"They sent me to Stettin to build fortifications against the Russians. But the military commander took one look at us and told the S.S. to take us back because we were more dead than alive.

"I was liberated in Belsen. I was in very bad shape, no longer able to walk. We received a package from the Red Cross, some hardtack and a can of condensed milk. I was liberated, the Germans were defeated, but all around me people were still dying, and I didn't have the strength even to open a can of milk. That was the first time in my life that I started to cry.

"A British soldier asked what I was doing. I showed him that I was trying to punch a hole in the can, and then I remembered my sister who went to England, and I asked whether he knew anybody in his outfit from that area. A few minutes later he came back with a nurse and an officer.

"The nurse was from Bedford where my sister was, and she wrote down my sister's name and the names of the people she stayed with. The officer was a physician, and he took away that can of milk, and picked me up and carried me to the nearest barracks, and made a clear space in one of those filthy bunk beds.

"He brought me a huge can of zweiback toast and a five-gallon can of English tea and he says, 'That's all you're gonna drink or eat if you want to stay alive. Don't move, and I'll come see you every day.' And he did. He saved my life.

"The British brought in German prisoners to carry the bodies and dump them into mass graves. Then they brought in bulldozers and set the camp on fire.

"A Swedish Red Cross official came to take down names of former inmates who were in bad shape, to be taken to Sweden. He asked each one their nationality, and when I said Austrian he said he can't take Germans or Austrians. I said, 'I was put into this mess because I am Jewish, not Austrian!' A day later I was on the ambulance train to Bremen and then went by ambulance boat to Sweden.

"I wanted to leave Europe behind me. In 1947 some friends helped me come to the United States. I stayed on the East Coast for about half a year and was on the verge of going back to Sweden when somebody told me, 'What you see here is not really the United States.' I found out there are Scandinavians in Minnesota, and I figured if they could stand the cold, maybe I could too!"

MURRAY BRANDYS

SOSNOWIEC, POLAND

"'What if I sing for the SS?' I asked. 'Do you think if I tell them that I will sing, they will let me go?' 'That won't help you now they said. I don't know what was going through my mind at that point, but I had nothing to lose. I opened my mouth and began to sing."

Murray Brandys spent most of his childhood on Dekerta Street in Sosnowiec. He was 14 when the war started. When he was liberated by the Americans he weighed 60 pounds. For many years he did not share his stories. He did not want to burden his family with tales of his horrific experience.

"I lived in #5, an apartment building, with my family, my parents and six siblings," said Murray. "I was the youngest. Hendel and Chaya, our parents, were both successful businesspeople. Our second-floor apartment was spacious and homey with three large rooms. Our neighborhood was in the midst of town, an area packed with apartment buildings and bustling shops.

"While our parents ran their businesses and my siblings were busy attending school, working and finding their mates, I was growing older, going to school and having fun. During the school week I attended a public Jewish elementary school from 8 a.m. to 3 p.m. I was an average student, but choir and soccer were my passions. After school I would attend cheder, or Hebrew school, until 6 p.m. While little free time existed, I loved spending time with my brothers and friends, singing in the choir and going to the movies.

"Family life also meant religious life. We attended a modern but Orthodox synagogue. After services, out-of-town visitors would stand outside the synagogue door waiting for an invitation from a local family to Shabbat dinner. Regardless of whether a visitor accompanied us home, always certain after services were two things: a generous, multicourse meal and an impromptu concert afterwards. So musical was our family that passersby would sometimes gather in our backyard to listen to us singing through open windows. Growing up, I dreamed of becoming a cantor or, more grandly, a conductor.

"I remember well the Sunday evening that was the end of my childhood and the beginning of a new life. September 1, 1939, the Germans invaded. German tanks rolled into town from the west, down the middle of the street, flanked on each side by marching soldiers. Town residents scattered into their apartment buildings, locking the doors behind them and ducking beneath windows as guns were fired.

"The German occupation of Sosnowiec brought both drastic and subtle changes to the Jews' lives there. Now we all wore yellow stars, identifying us as Jews. Synagogues were destroyed or seized. Jewish businesses, including my parents' were shut down. With no jobs and no real freedoms, my father and mother stayed at home. One day, we heard a knock, my father opened the door and there stood two German soldiers. They ordered us to leave while they took an inventory of our possessions. We had little choice but to go. The soldiers took nearly all of our possessions including our piano. They left us our beds and a couch.

"Not long after our possessions were seized, my life dramatically changed. It was a spring day, roughly eight months since the German invasion, and I was walking along Targowa Street near my house, when suddenly German trucks blocked both ends of the street. Every man and boy, Jew and Gentile alike, was ordered into the trucks and driven to a large building a couple of miles away. Quickly the Gentiles were separated from the Jews and sent home. But we Jews, old and young, were kept overnight, refused food and placed on a train the next morning. I would never again see my father and mother, my sisters or two of my brothers.

"Eventually, our train stopped near Breslau, Germany. By now, filled with fear and still unfed, we 30 men and boys stumbled off the train into Sakrau, a small forced-labor camp. Their first order was forcing us to strip so they could make sure that we weren't hiding jewelry or gold. Then they took our clothing, gave us striped uniforms, and sent us to the disinfecting showers. The second morning we were sent into town to begin digging ditches along the street curb.

"The next stop was Czyniec, a divided forced

Murray Brandys

labor camp, with one side for Jews, the other for French Christians. Surviving Czyniec was much more difficult than Sakrau. Here our work meant taking apart an old steel mill, removing brick after brick and placing them in railroad cars. Our daily meal was one quarter-pound of bread and some thin soup with vegetables. If the prisoner in charge of the soup liked you, you might get more vegetables. This rarely happened for me.

"I remember one sunny Sunday morning sitting on the grass singing—singing for self-preservation. I kept hoping for a better day, which seemed nearly impossible. But if I didn't have hope, I knew I would never survive. After a long time, I'm guessing more than a year. I was sent to Hundsfeld. While my previous camps were forced labor camps, I knew immediately that this was a concentration camp. Hitler's Secret Service reigned supreme here, calling us Untermenschen or Sub-humans. The Judenselster (Jewish prisoner in charge of the prisoners) was from my hometown. Luckily for me, he knew I could sing and would request that I visit their barracks on Sunday nights to perform for them and the kapos.

"About 50 of us were again sent by train to a concentration camp in Hirschberg. There most prisoners worked at a paper factory across the street from the camp. I didn't work at the paper mill. I was sent on a daily 45-minute hike to a building development. There we were building houses for German families. Strange as it may seem, I continued to sing, sometimes for myself, sometimes for the kapo, both individually and with a group.

"At the end of 1944, the order came to evacuate Hirschberg. By then I had been imprisoned four years and was eighteen years old. My next destination was Buchenwald, a huge city of brick buildings. It was the first time I was branded by a number. Monick was no more. From then on, I would be referred to only by 133909.

"We began a death march in early April walking day after day guarded by S.S. They directed us to walk mostly through forests so American planes wouldn't spot us. It had been a couple of weeks and I kept pushing on. A friend of mine marched directly across from me. I remember it was late in the afternoon and the sun was going down. That's when my friend, completely exhausted, just stopped in his tracks and laid down. The rest of us didn't pause but kept going. People walked right over him. I heard the shot and knew he was dead.

"I always kept a look out for food. One day, I spotted something five feet from the wagon, something that looked like food. I thought if I was quick. I might not be noticed. I ran to pick it up but an S.S. officer saw me and dragged me to the Death Commando. Two of them held my arms so that I could not run back to the prisoner line. I knew I'd soon be shot in the forest. This was to be the end. But I still had hope.

"I addressed the two men holding me. 'What if I sing for the SS?' I asked. 'Do you think if I tell them that I will sing, they will let me go?' 'That won't help you now,' they said. I don't know what was going through my mind at that point, but I had nothing to lose. I opened my mouth and began to sing. I sang for maybe two minutes. I don't know what song I sang, something in Yiddish, maybe a folk song. But it was the solo of my life. For whatever reason, the executioner listened to my song and then ordered the Death Commando to send me back to the line of prisoners. My life had been saved."

Condensed from "My Name Was No 133909" by Murray Brandys

Reprinted with permission from the website of the Center for Holocaust & Genocide Studies at the University of Minnesota

MARGOT DEWILDE

BERLIN, GERMANY

"The smell of Auschwitz was overpowering. A terrible, burning smell permeated the air."

Every year Margot held one day sacred—May 5th, 1945, the day she was liberated from the Nazis.

Ruth Margot Lustig was born into a privileged life. Her grandfather was the owner of a large department store where her father worked. In Berlin, toys, books, music, and art, as well as a large extended family, surrounded Margot. With the decline of the German economy in the mid-1920's her family's financial situation declined.

The store closed and Margot's father search for work took him to Amsterdam. Although Margot continued to live in Berlin with her mother and brother, it became increasingly evident to her mother that the city was no longer safe for Jewish families. Demonstrations, riots and the rise of the Hitler Youth frightened her. In 1932, when Margot was almost eleven years old, the family was able to leave Berlin and join her father in Amsterdam.

By 1938 when Margot met Lodewyk Meyer, the man she would marry, the situation for Jews in Germany was dire. Hitler continued to pose more and more restrictions on the Jews. All Jewish citizens were required to wear the yellow star, they were restricted access to stores and banned from public transportation. Jewish students were expelled from German schools and Jewish property was confiscated.

However, the Jews of Holland were not affected by the changes taking place in Germany until May 10, 1940 when Germany invaded Holland. Soon the Jews of Holland were under the same restrictions as the German Jews. Despite the requirement to wear the yellow star, Margot continued to go about her daily life without wearing the star. But as the situation for Jews deteriorated, Margot and her husband decided to leave Holland for the United States. Unfortunately their papers arrived on December 7, 1941, the day the Japanese bombed Pearl Harbor and all immigration to the United States was halted.

By 1941 the deportation of Jews from Holland had

Margot DeWilde

begun. Margot's parents and her brother received papers to report for deportation, but went into hiding. Margot decided to work with the Dutch Resistance. She spoke fluent German and did not "look Jewish." She worked with the Underground producing false identification papers and, because of her Aryan looks, was able to pass among the citizens to distribute these false documents.

In 1943 Margot and her husband received news that they could escape to Switzerland. But they were betrayed. They were pulled off the train in Cologne and sent to Berlin where they were detained with other Jews. After several days Margot became very ill and had to be hospitalized. When she rejoined her husband, they learned that they were again being relocated. This time their destination was be Auschwitz. "The smell of Auschwitz was overpowering. A terrible, burning smell permeated the air," remembered Margot.

The day Margot arrived in Auschwitz, Dr. Josef Mengele, known as the Angel of Death, made a special selection. "We had to separate right away on the train platform. Mengele, who was there to direct the people, had the young married women step forward, and I was a young married woman so I stepped forward. We were taken to the sauna first, to the shower. And we had to get out of our clothes. They shaved our hair. Then we were taken to a barracks which turned out to be a medical experiment barracks, where we were tattooed." From that time on she was no longer Ruth Margot Lustig Meyer, but number 47574.

After her assignment to Barrack 10, Margot soon learned from another inmate that she and the others would be subjects of human experiments. She did not know that many who were led to the experiment rooms were never seen again. She was subjected to sterilization experiments.

During her imprisonment she was also given a job so she received extra rations. While working in the camp's infirmary she found her husband who had developed tuberculosis. "It spared him from going to the gas chamber," said Margot. "Three times he was on the death list, but he died of natural causes in his bunk, in April 1944. I was raised Orthodox, but when he died, I started to ask why he died. I couldn't believe anymore." From Auschwitz Margot was transferred to Ravensbruck. "From there I went on a death march, fleeing the Russians. That's where I was liberated."

Every year Margot held one day sacred—May 5th, the day she was liberated from the Nazis. "There was shooting and commotion all around. And I had suggested somebody should stay awake who could speak Russian. I could speak English and I stayed up that night in case somebody came and we could explain who we were, that we were not Germans, that we were prisoners. I saw a prisoner with a prison suit walking with an American flag. And I thought, 'My God, keep your mouth shut, you're hallucinating. It is wishful thinking.' But then some prisoners came in and said. 'Get out, you're free!' That was our liberation."

PAULETTE FINK

PARIS, FRANCE

"My husband said, 'We are not going to run away. We are going to stay here and fight.' We fought almost five years with the French Underground. Then my husband was caught and tortured to death."

Paulette Weill's husband was a wealthy businessman. Her father had been a spy for France during World War I, and she and her husband joined the Resistance when France fell. After the war, she set up orphanages for Jewish children and helped smuggle refugees into Palestine.

"My mother had absolutely no religious training, and as far as our home was concerned, we had no tradition, but my husband was the grandson of the chief rabbi of Paris," said Paulette Fink. "He had fantastic pride as a Jew and a fantastic desire to be respected as a Jew. I never had any experience with anti-Semitism, never heard that I was 'different.' I had as many non-Jewish friends as Jewish ones. Then I was in Germany the end of 1932, and at the swimming pool a sign at the door said, 'No Dogs, No Jews.' A couple we knew arrived from Vienna in 1937, and I remember them telling us the Nazis were giving Jewish girls toothbrushes and making them clean the yard of the military barracks. I'm not sure how much we believed. Besides, that was Germany, Austria. That couldn't happen in France!

45

Paulette Fink (center) with daughters Francelyne Lurie (left) and Naidene Beecher (right)

"My parents had rented a house on the southern coast of Brittany, and that's where the war caught us. When the Germans came through the Belgian border and into Paris in seven days, we were in shock. My husband was a lieutenant in the army, and he was taken prisoner. I was on the front line as a Red Cross nurse, and I didn't know where he was. But he escaped four times from a prisoner-of-war camp and finally made it the fourth time.

"We were under the control of Marshal Petain in Vichy, in so-called Free France. He had sold out to the Germans, betrayed his countrymen. One of Petain's big lies was that if you were French for more than five generations, you had nothing to risk by declaring yourself. So we all declared ourselves at the police station. We were never compelled to wear the Star of David like they did in the occupied zone, but we were trapped.

"The French Resistance started when General de Gaulle spoke on the BBC from London, appealing to the French people to fight, sabotage, infiltrate, do everything we could to stop the German war machine. We could very easily have joined my parents in Morocco, but for my husband, de Gaulle was a g od.

"Leaders discover themselves. My husband, who was proprietor of a big chain of five-and-ten-cent stores, used one of his stores for a headquarters. In his store he had tons of dried beans, lentils, green peas, and he put an ad in the newspaper saying, 'Monday morning, food will be distributed. Free.' On Monday thousands queued up, but ration cards had been started, and the authorities arrested him!

"I was terribly scared. I knew Marshal Petain—I had met him at my sister's wedding—and I went to him, and he said, 'What can I do for you, my child?' I told him point-blank, 'You can give the order to release my husband.' He said, 'My poor child, I am so sorry. If only you weren't Jewish I could help you.' In Vichy we had a few men who were working a double game, and I was able to find such a man. He was very cold, very suspicious, but he finally called the fortress. and said, 'This is Marshal Petain's office. You are ordered to release so-and-so.' And that night my husband was out!

"There were no trains, no cars, no gas. For a little while I had a car; they'd put an enormous tank in the back, and we were burning wood to run the car. But then we began bicycling everywhere. I was my husband's message carrier. I once bicycled over 200 kilometers—almost 125 miles!

"My husband's store had yards and yards of a kind of denim, really mattress ticking, and if I gave a farmer enough to make a suit, he would give me butter and eggs and milk. The main thing was not to be arrested on the road going back, because if the Germans found you with even half a pound of potatoes, they put you in jail!

"My husband organized a quartermaster corps to provide food, blankets, shirts, pants, tents, everything, to the Resistance. We were getting money from Algiers to help mothers and children when the husband was gone. We were also getting bandages and American cigarettes. We had a friend who got picked up because he was having a cup of coffee at the bistro and he left an American cigarette butt in the ashtray. Another friend and his brother were in an apartment with two entrances, an obvious entrance with the number on the door, and a back entrance nobody could find. They had planned for years that they would run out the second door if somebody came. But one day, somebody knocked and impulsively one brother went to the door. And that was the end for them. It's the things you never expected that tripped you up. We were all afraid of being denounced. All we needed was to be recognized by one guy from the French *milice* who had been trained by the Gestapo.

"We lived in many places. One was this gorgeous abandoned castle near

47

Grenoble. Thank God for the fireplace. All fourteen of us would sit there by that fireplace, keeping warm, my two little daughters doing schoolwork.

"I don't remember the many names I used in the Resistance. To change identification cards was very tricky, not just picking a name. We had an entire network of people finding names of people who were in mental hospitals or had just died—all far away from where we lived, of course. We'd get the entire pedigree of that person, so that if the Germans caught you, you knew the answers.

"Each of us also had an Underground name. Whenever they called on the radio for Walnut Tree, for example, you'd know it was you. We had to be very careful because the Germans had electronic devices on their cars and picked up people who were taking the message.

"Sometimes we got parachute drops, parts of machine guns, but then sometimes we didn't get the second part of the guns because the Germans got the message before we did. We also picked up paratroopers—Canadians and Americans who were carriers of messages—and we hid them. We had an entire network of volunteers who were saving children. France was full of Jewish refugees from Poland, Hungary, Romania. A big trick of the Germans was to leave children at the railroad station when they packed the parents in railroad cars to take them to the camps. They knew these little children would be lost because they knew nobody, didn't speak French. They spoke only Yiddish, and none of us understood them.

"We kept a record of all the children we got. Their names, their parents' names if we knew them, where they were hidden. I don't remember having any children younger than about two because the mothers were usually carrying babies in their arms when they boarded the trains. We passed the children from one to another to hide them, a chain with many links—priests and nuns, monasteries and convents, Catholic schools, some on farms to work as farmhands with no pay. The Catholics were fabulous, the Protestants too. In Le Chambon, Pastor Trocme and his people were always willing to help.

"After D-Day, after the sixth of June 1944, de Gaulle and Eisenhower told the Resistance, 'Go out, work in the open, do as much harm to the Germans as you possibly can.' My husband did, and he got caught. A friend came to me with the bad news. I immediately went into the garage to get on my bicycle and said, 'I'm going.' But he said, 'You cannot go where he is, it's not possible. Every mile is full of Germans,' so I didn't go. When we were liberated August 14, I took my children and went to find him.

"But he had been killed on June 24 and buried as 'Unknown.' Because he was carrying so many false names, they didn't know his real name. They wanted me to identify him, but I refused to look. He had been tortured for over twelve hours, and I didn't want to remember him that way.

"When the war ended, to see the Germans sitting at the cafe that morning, and in the afternoon the Americans was unbelievable. But we got food, K-rations. Today I wouldn't even open one of those cans of Spam, but then it tasted so good! I got involved with children's homes. I spoke English fluently, so I went to see the head of the Jewish Joint Distribution Committee. I told him we knew of hundreds of Jewish children that we could get back. We could requisition homes from the government. But we needed money. He looked at me and said, 'Well, Madame, prove what you can do and we'll help.' And I did.

"I made debts everywhere. At every grocery store, I promised to pay at the end of the month, and they didn't want to let those children starve. We 'requisitioned' a big house, and by hook and crook we found cots and mattresses. We raided a furniture warehouse one night and stole one of the JDC trucks to carry the stuff! We had done much worse than that in the Resistance! But when the social workers told some of those children that their name was Goldberg and not Smith, and that they were Jewish, the kids didn't believe they were Jewish, they didn't want to be Jewish. So we kidnapped them. We found a Jewish woman who taught the kids Yiddish songs. We wanted them to feel some Jewishness, and none of us could do that. And little by little, the kids gave up their reticence.

"Their parents would never come back, but many didn't believe us. Some refused to go to school, refused to go out of the house, in case their parents came to look for them. All the children were registered at a center in Paris— name, address, parents' names, where they would be in case somebody came looking for them.

"We soon had eleven houses, 1,500 kids. At the end of 1945 I went to the JDC and said, 'I can't continue. Americans send me some shoes, but only sixty pairs for a hundred children. Which children will get the shoes?' So he looked at me and said, 'You go to America and see what you can do.' I came for three months, with my daughter Nadine. She was nine years old, and when we went into the dining room on the ship, she looked at the enormous platter of cold cuts and cheeses and fruits, and she started to cry. We didn't have ration cards, and she couldn't believe there was such a thing as getting food without a coupon. I covered forty-two states, making speeches, and I got the money I needed.

"One night. back in Paris, at about two in the morning, there's a knock at the door. I open my window and I see men. On their arms I see the words 'Palestine Brigade.' I have no idea who they are. They had almost 200 refugees illegally on their way to Palestine and they wanted to leave them with me overnight. They had in their trucks a double bottom full of guns, and they wanted to go to Marseille, unload their guns, and then come back to take the people to an illegal boat they were expecting.

"We had two children's homes at that time on the outskirts of Paris. It was the other house that had been notified these people were coming, but they came to me by mistake. What do I do? I said yes.

"When the guys came back, I went with them to help. We found the place on the beach, and we put those people in inflated rubber boats, ten at a time, with one strong man to hold the rope. The rope was a link between the beach and the boat, two or three miles away. It was pitch black, no moon and no stars, and the people were holding that rope and walking into complete darkness, in January, in that bitterly cold water.

"I worked with the Breichah from Italy, from Austria. We started emptying the displaced person camps long before we were given permission. Then the State of Israel was created, and refugees could immigrate. I went back and forth to America for eight years, raising money for Israel. I brought my children to the United States in 1951. At last they were able to lead a normal life."

ROBERT O. FISCH

BUDAPEST, HUNGARY

"We had to walk from Graz to Mauthausen. Sometimes we didn't get anything to eat or drink. An Austrian peasant threw us apples and a

German guard shot the peasant. One day we saw a lot more bodies than usual. One S.S. sergeant just decided he was going to shoot every fifth person in line!"

Robert O. Fisch wanted to be an artist or an architect when he grew up, but when he was released from Mauthausen at age twenty he went home and enrolled in medical school. During the Hungarian revolution in 1957 he treated both wounded Russian soldiers and the Hungarian schoolboys who were fighting against them.

"My grandfather came to Hungary from Poland when he was six years old," said Fisch. "He was very poor, but he went to the amusement park and got a bucket and started to sell water. Later he and my father got geese, chickens, ducks and sold them to market, and became very wealthy in the poultry business.

"We lived among Catholics, and I had Jewish and non-Jewish friends. The most dear person to me as I grew up was a Catholic woman who had been with us since I was eight months of age. She eventually had a great role in our lives because her parents were hiding my mother during the German occupation, although to help Jewish people was risking their own lives.

"History, unfortunately, never avoided Hungary. When Germany invaded Russia, the Hungarians were on the side of the Germans but by 1944 the Germans had lost their winning start and the Russians were coming. So on March 19 the Germans officially occupied Hungary even though the Hungarians were supposed to be their allies!

"The Germans established a Jewish advisors group for communication with the Jewish community. We had to wear a yellow star on our coats, ten centimeters in diameter. University student demonstrators were openly anti-Jewish. About ten days after the Germans occupied Hungary, I was in the building that was the center of the Jewish religious community, and a very upset person arrived. I sneaked into the room and listened. He described deportations taking place in the villages, how they go to the outside of the village, every Jewish person, with a little bag of clothes and food. In freight cars with room for twenty people they put 100 people, without any water, locked them in, and the train eventually went somewhere. From then on, I

Robert O. Fisch

had no expectations from the Germans, except to be killed.

"June 5, 1944, I was sent to a work camp to build bridges. We were some 240 men in that camp. They were taking away our photographs, and they tore the pictures and said, 'You're never going to see your family.' We had to work very hard, but we were reasonably well fed. My parents brought a radio to me, so we were able to listen to the BBC, and with maps we followed very precisely what was taking place. We knew the war was going to be ending, and the Germans had no way to win. We were called to dig out unexploded bombs, but when we saw the American air force flying, we knew that every bomb they dropped was our freedom.

"In January 1945, we were moved out. We came to this brick burner, and suddenly a smell hit me. Inside were hundreds of dead and dying people, bone and skin, defecating, full of lice, unable even to sit up. We were forced to sleep three nights among these people.

"Then they took us by train to the Austrian border, and we stayed in a little village, digging ditches to defend Austria against the Russians. When we arrived, they gave us one loaf of bread for every five of us. A German military man actually tried to help, and gave us one bread for every three men. Some S.S. also hid food behind their coats and gave it to us. One guy was hitting and kicking people, even women and children, and one day I was assigned to him, and I was so scared, but when we got out in the forest he said, 'Relax, sit down,' and gave us food. Then when we went back, he started to scream and hit people again.

"One day a person just collapsed. They started to kick him, and then they recognized that something was wrong. From the lice in the brick burner we had gotten typhoid, it was a typhoid epidemic! From the end of January until May, more than half the men died. I was very young and I was in extremely good physical shape, but I was running a high temperature. The Germans established a room for sick people and one day an S.S. truck came, and they said the twenty sickest individuals could go to the hospital, that the food was wonderful. I didn't trust the Germans, but one of my friends went. They were all shot at the edge of the village.

"We walked from there to Graz, an industrial area. If someone was not able to walk, they shot him right there. In the mornings, some of us threw our blankets away, and in the afternoons picked things up from the dead, so we wouldn't have to carry the blankets all day.

"Mauthausen was a political camp and also a military prison. There were some American prisoners there. Ten decagrams of bread —about one-fourth of a pound —with fungus on it, and one cup of coffee was our food for the whole day. The next day we were taken to Gunskirchen, a sub-camp. They put us in a long wooden building. We had to sit on the ground, with people leaning on our knees, with somebody sitting next to us and behind us. When people started to fall sleep or tried to lie down, they lay on other people. Many people died, just suffocated.

"We had to stand in line every morning, noon, and evening to be counted. For six hours we were in line, twelve hours we were in the barracks, and the rest we could go to the bathroom. For 30,000 prisoners they had two bathrooms. One day I could not wait for my turn, so I just urinated in the field. A German guard saw me and beat me with his rifle.

"Our food was usually bitter coffee, a little bread, a little soup. The Jewish kapos were very cruel. They had food, and we hated them so. One day we received something extraordinary, an International Red Cross gift, little food packages, and these kapos were eating whole bars of chocolate while fifty people had to divide a can of sardines and six lumps of sugar. If I had the opportunity, I would have killed them to get that chocolate away from them.

"The American army came on May 4, in the evening. I was so weak I had to crawl up the stairway. Liberation was incredible, chaotic. The Americans

WITNESSES TO THE HOLOCAUST

threw us food, candies, everything they had. American medical people tried to help us, but we were dehydrated, starving. I'm a doctor, and I don't know what I could do with this kind of situation. It was absolutely unreal. The American army knew the Germans very well, and yet they asked us what happened to us, why were we here? They could not believe the Germans were doing this only because someone had a different religion.

"The Americans took us to the Russian zone. It was still about thirty miles to the next railroad, so I stayed overnight in a little ruined home. I had some liquor to take to my father, and a Russian soldier said he would like to buy it. I said, 'Fine, give me some money or take me to the railroad.' An hour later he came back with a machine gun!

"I also had some cigarettes and was able to buy a ride to the next railroad station with them. So that's how I got home. With the help of Raoul Wallenberg and some Russians, 50,000 of the 100,000 Jews in the ghetto were saved, but my father and all my relatives in small towns had been killed. My brother had left before the occupation to study engineering in Switzerland, and my mother was hidden by our Catholic friend, so they were saved. They immigrated to Israel, but I stayed in Budapest in medical school.

"When the Communists took over after the war, it was as bad as under the Nazis. Then in 1956 we had a revolution. I watched the Russian tanks coming into Budapest, and Hungarian students, twelve years old some of them, holding hands and marching against the tanks. We organized to provide medical assistance for the revolutionaries.

"I had heard they had medical supplies at the Austrian border. So we stole four trucks from a government garage, put red crosses on them, and started west to the border. We saw a caravan coming, French, American, English relatives of embassy people fleeing into Austria. So we broke into the caravan, and with these foreign diplomats we went to the border.

"The Austrian border guards were very friendly and we went on to Vienna. Outside Vienna the Austrian police waited for us, and the chief said, 'You cannot go any further. Ask for political asylum, or go back to Hungary.'

"I knew it was the craziest thing to go back to Hungary, but we packed the trucks with medical supplies and food and went back to the hospital, which was now the communication center for the Hungarian revolution. Then the revolution was over. How stupid I had been to go back. Many people were being executed. I lost weight, I didn't look too good, and a doctor friend recommended that I go to a sanitarium near the Austrian border. There I said to the doctors, 'I want to get out,' and they brought someone who led me to the border. In 1958 I came to New York.

"When the war ended, I had a lot of hatred in me, and I thought I would be able to be cruel to the Germans. But when I met Germans who were hungry, I had two choices. I could either do the same things they did to me, or I could be different. And I didn't feel that to make them suffer was the answer."

CHARLES FODOR

BUDAPEST, HUNGARY

"The Danube froze that January and the Russians crossed the Danube to liberate the city. It was the first time the river had frozen in many years. The Russians came from the west side, moving toward the ghetto, eventually liberating us."

On the banks of the Danube River in Budapest visitors today find 60 pairs of iron shoes: men's shoes, women's shoes, and children's shoes. They memorialize the days when the river ran red with Jewish blood, as Jewish citizens of Budapest were taken to the riverbank and shot by members of the Hungarian fascists, the Arrow Cross.

In mid-May 1944, as Hungarian authorities, in coordination with the German Security Police, began to systematically deport the Hungarian Jews, Charles Fodor was only eight years old. In less than two months, nearly 440,000 Hungarian Jews were deported. "November 11, 1944, my mother was taken away to work in Austria, and she never came back," said Charles.

By the end of July 1944, the only Jewish community left in Hungary was in the capital, Budapest. All the Jewish citizens were required to live in apartment houses that posted the names of its Jewish residents on the front next to a yellow star, and all Jewish residents were required to wear the yellow star. "My grandmother and I, and my grandparents' cousins and aunts received letters of protection when the Swiss, the Portuguese and the Swedes began providing these letters to Jews who applied for them. Temporarily, we lived in what was called the International Ghetto."

While the Budapest ghetto was formed in June 1944, the neutral states planned a rescue action for the Jews of Budapest. In July 1944, Raoul Wallenberg came to Budapest as secretary of the Swedish Foreign Ministry with instructions to save as many Jews as possible. He worked with the Swiss consul Charles Lutz, as well as the Portuguese and Spanish legations, to create a "protected ghetto" to house the Jews with international identity papers.

"I remember one thing that happened as my grandmother and I were going to the house which was under the international protection," said Charles. At the Danube River we were blocked and stopped by three women wearing armbands with an Arrow Cross It was the Hungarian fascists. And they ordered us into a big apartment building on the Grand Boulevard, by the Danube River. As we walked in, we saw a man bending over toward the basement and we didn't know what was going on until later. A man was coming out of the building and he grabbed my grandmother and me and said, 'You don't belong in here. Come with me.' He led us away from the fascists, around the block, and said, 'Get lost.'" It was later they learned that all those in the building were taken out and murdered on the banks of the Danube River.

The Hungarian fascist Arrow Cross Party was responsible for carrying out many violent attacks against the Jews. The Arrow Cross would sometimes line Jews up along the Danube and shoot them so they fell into the river in order to avoid burying the bodies. Victims were made to remove their shoes prior to being shot because their shoes had value to the Nazis.

By January 18th the war in Hungary was over. "I was in Budapest," said Charles. "The Danube froze that January and the Russians crossed the Danube to liberate the city. It was the first time the river had frozen in many years. The Russians came from the west side, moving toward the ghetto, eventually liberating us."

The international ghetto was liberated by the Soviets on January 16, 1945, and the central ghetto two days later. About 94,000 Jews remained in the two ghettos at the time of liberation. Another 20,000 came out of hiding from the city, and another 20,000 returned from labor camps and labor service detachments. Nearly fifty percent of Budapest's Jewish population died during the Holocaust.

Charles' father had been conscripted into the Hungarian military. "A lot of Hungarian Jewish men, in the early stages of the war, were wearing Hungarian uniforms with a yellow armband saying that they're Jewish. They were guarded by the Hungarian military with bayonets. They built roads and bridges and were

Charles Fodor

used as living mine detectors on the Russian front. Later, in civilian clothes, they dug ditches under guard with the labor battalions. My father was in a labor battalion on the Russian front and he escaped from the Hungarians. He was caught by the Russians, escaped from the Russians, and then came back to Budapest two days behind the Russians. So he survived.

"I grew up in Hungary. In 1956, Hungarians had an uprising against the Russians, and the result was that the Iron Curtain came down for about 200,000 Hungarians. The United States government had a special immigration quota and I was part of the first 5,000 who got a green card and came as an immigrant to the United States."

Charles Fodor speaks to school groups about his childhood hiding from the Nazis, and his youth under Communism. He has a message for his audience. "Do a mitzvah—a good deed—each day, and thank God for the gift of life."

HENRY FREIER

LODZ, POLAND

"In the ghetto, when one father's son died, he kept the body in the cellar for weeks, to collect the boy's rations. I was there. I saw it, I smelled it. How can you forget something like that?"

Taunted from childhood by Polish boys saying "Your houses, our streets," eighteen-year-old Henry Freier, whose father was an ardent Zionist, set out for Palestine in 1932. He and four teenage friends hitchhiked to the Italian coast but were turned back by the British authorities.

"We were eight children at home," said Henry, "and I was the oldest boy. I was eleven when I quit school and started working where my father worked as manager for an office supply company. Every penny I made was to help feed my siblings.

"In 1939 Polish radio announced, 'We won't give the Germans even a button from our coats.' The newspaper in Lodz said, 'Our Polish heroes are forty kilometers from Berlin.' But in ten days the war was over.

"In our building there were seventeen Polish families and seven Jewish families. I was born and raised with one guy, a Catholic. I used to go with him to church. I was a boxer, and we belonged to the same sport club. But two days after the German army came to Lodz, this man was wearing a swastika. He said, 'Don't talk to me. My grandmother was German.'

"To get 300,000 people into the ghetto, every 'Volksdeutscher' and German was chasing, beating and even killing us. I was twenty-five and married. I got a horse and buggy to move my furniture, and they took the furniture, the horse, the buggy, and the guy I hired to help me, too. Our apartment in the ghetto was one room. My wife and I slept in one bed and in the other bed slept my wife's sisters. Bathrooms were outside.

"In the beginning in the ghetto, we had concerts. We had very good musicians. We had intellectuals and there were schools, but not for long. I opened a little store selling cheese, butter, smuggled food. One morning the police came and took everything from the store. They beat me so hard I could hardly move. My wife ran to a very prominent man in the ghetto, officially a Gestapo agent but I knew him from before the war, and he saved my life.

"Then I became a 'watchman.' My job was to watch the potatoes. We had people digging out the potatoes, covering them with straw and putting sand on them, so the rations would last through the winter. One October day many tons of potatoes came in but at night came a frost. The potatoes froze and rotted. But people were starving and they were eating those rotten potatoes. You could see people in the ghetto crawling on all fours, swollen from hunger.

"Then came the first evacuation. They started with the children and the hospitals. Next, 66,000 Jews were evacuated. They took them on trucks to Chelmno. They told us these people were going to work, but I saw my Catholic friend in the ghetto, and he said to me, 'Henry, they are killing your brothers and sisters in Chelmno.' And when their belongings came back, we knew they didn't go to work.

"I witnessed one episode, a beautiful blond Jewish woman with a daughter eleven years old. They took the daughter because she didn't have a work certificate. The girl was screaming, 'Mama, help me!' and the mother ran to this Nazi and started kissing his dirty boots. He kneeled down and raised her by her beautiful blond hair, and he put a bullet in her brain.

"When we were taken in 1944 to Auschwitz Birkenau, men who knew me were unloading the trains. Old people were sent one way with the children, the men another way, the women another way. My friends saw my wife carrying our baby, and they said to me, 'Henry, quick, take the baby from your wife and give him to an old woman because your child is going right into the fire with whoever's carrying him.' We did, and they threw my son and the old woman who was carrying him right into the fire.

"I was digging, pushing wagons with sand, building highways. In the ghetto I had given a man an apartment with furniture, and in Auschwitz this same man was our kapo, the man who decided death or life for us. So he brought me bread, and he said, 'You're not going out to work.' My job was to watch in front of the barracks, and if an S.S. guard walked by, I let the kapos know. I also made sure that nobody ran to the electric wires to commit suicide.

"From Auschwitz, about 2000 of us were sent to Grossrosen. As we passed the women's camp, I saw my sister and my wife. It was the last time I saw them.

"On the train to Grossrosen, we didn't have food for three days. When we got there we got a little bit of soup and a few slices of bread, and they said this was to last for twenty-four hours. I finished it almost with one bite. We went to sleep on bare boards.

"In the morning a kapo selected men to work in the kitchen. I said I was a butcher because next to me was a real butcher I knew from Lodz. The meat was horse meat, hanging quarters. A butcher knows how to unhook and take the meat on his shoulder, and I didn't, but the kapo let the real butcher show me how to do it and how to cut the meat from the bone. The meat was for the S.S., the bones went into soup for us. I was the cook for the S.S. guard, making meat, potatoes and thick soup. I ate the meat, too, and I would steal the thick soup and bring it to the sickroom. The kapo called me 'his Jew.' I was beaten by this man every day. First he beat me up, then he fed me. That's the way it was.

"I was very healthy and stronger than most of the others. I was one of only six men who were never ill. Some of the people I knew from Lodz were still with me, and a doctor from Lodz died in my arms. Before he died, he took out his upper plate of false teeth—platinum —and said, 'Henry, take this. Maybe this platinum will save your life.' And it later did.

"I was in Grossrosen until 1945. The Soviet armies were five kilometers away, and we heard shooting day and night. Only 600 of the 2,000 men from Lodz were still alive. They collected everybody from all the camps in the area, and marched us first one place, then another. We were walking through a town when I heard a German woman ask an S.S. guard, 'Who are those people in the stripes?' The guard said, 'Jews.' She said, 'Why don't you kill them?'

"We were on trains for nine days, sitting on dead bodies. We wound up in Flossenburg. Of 8,000 people in the train, there were 3,000 bodies. The bodies were green, falling to pieces. The smell was indescribable. The crematorium could take only so many, so we had to dig ditches and put in wood and tar and people, wood and tar and people. It was cold, drizzling, mud up to our knees. People were dying like flies.

"I had these platinum teeth, and I said to the guard in charge, 'This is worth a lot of money. Take it.' He asked me what I wanted, so I said 'Don't chase me out to work at three in the morning, and I want my good friend to work with me.' So we got to work where the transports came in and they took away all the clothes. Our job was to look through the clothes for money and valuables. The guards, kapos, everybody danced around us, this one needs socks, another needs a pair of pants, they gave us orders. We brought things to them and they fed us.

"From Flossenburg we went to Regensburg. There we were cleaning up, picking up bodies where the Americans were bombing. Every day we lost fifty or sixty men, hungry, sick, shot by the guards.

One day the chef picked me up to go to the butcher shop. I had in my striped prisoner uniform a pocket I had sewn inside, and I put a piece of sausage in my pocket. A German guard, the worst killer, found out and took me down to the end of the line. If they take you to the end of the line, it's to death, but my brother-in-law ran to the cook, who ran to one of the officers, who came running and pushed the rifle, and the bullet went into the ground instead of into me. That was April 28, 1945.

"We were 150 guys from Lodz, still together, sick with typhus, but we knew Hitler was dead and the Americans were coming. The S.S. guard ran away, and we hid for two days. Then I saw American tanks, and I jumped on the first tank, and there were tears, and singing, and hugging.

"We took some revenge. We attacked one of the worst killers from the S.S. guard, killed him and buried him right there in Regensburg. Later, in Laufen, I was president of the Jewish committee, taking food from the Germans and distributing it to the Jews. It made me feel good. I was also working for the military government apprehending S.S. and war criminals.

"My dead wife's niece found out where I was, found my brother in the Polish army, and found her sister, now my wife, in Mauthausen. In 1949 I came to the United States."

PETER GERSH

MIECHOW, POLAND

"Many times in the middle of the night, I scream. I lived through the Holocaust and I still can't believe it. You have to try and live a normal life, but you can't forget."

Peter Gersh was eighteen when the Germans occupied Poland. He and his family were Orthodox Jews, and he belonged to a Zionist youth movement. He was a skilled mechanic who could repair cars and trucks, and he learned how to shoe horses. These were survival skills during the Nazi occupation.

"My parents, grandparents, great-grandparents were all born in Wlodzislaw," said Peter, "where nine out of ten were Jews. Tailors, shoemakers, capmakers, all were Jews, and Jewish doctors, dentists, lawyers. My father was the town's machinist and locksmith, and we employed at times up to ten non-Jews.

"News from Germany about the treatment of the Jews grew bleaker from day to day. Skirmishes between German and Polish border guards became more frequent. We were expecting war, and on August 31, 1939, our world stopped and everybody tuned in to the radio, waiting. September 1, early in the morning, the Polish president read a proclamation: 'Last night our mortal enemies, the Germans, crossed our borders. We are determined to repulse the attack.' That was wishful thinking. On September 7 the Germans marched into Miechow. September 10 the Polish army collapsed and Poland was under German control. My older brother and I and a few friends set out on foot to escape to Russia. But we were overtaken by a German motorized division about 150 miles east of Miechow, and there was nothing to do but return.

"For the first two or three months, it wasn't too bad because the Wehrmacht was in control. Then they handed their power over to the Gestapo, the local Polish police, and the Volksdeutsch. A few streets around the synagogue were set aside for a ghetto. They put walls up and barbed wire. There would not have been enough room for all of us, but they killed the elders and small children. The Germans promised the Poles free sugar for exposing Jews in hiding—sugar was in short supply and every day Jews were turned in and killed. Lack of food and medicine also took their toll.

"I had a dozen helpers, all Jews, and we worked fifteen to eighteen hours every day taking care of German cars and trucks. It gave us food to survive, and I could keep my family together. Then, in July 1942 they marched all the remaining Jews to the train station and loaded us into boxcars. The young and strong were sent to labor camps. The rest went to Belzec to be exterminated. My father was a professional, so he was spared. My brother was a tailor, which they needed also, and my younger brother worked with me.

"We had no doubt about what was awaiting the Jews in Poland. It was time to try to save whoever we could. For men that was almost impossible. They could recognize us as Jews because of circumcision. But with a little help and luck, some women could save themselves.

"We met a man from Germany who was a construction engineer in Cracow, forty kilometers away. He found a place with a family for my mother and the older of my two sisters. I got false papers for my mother and sister,

Peter Gersh (7th from left) with survivors of death march from Buchenwald to Dachau

WITNESSES TO THE HOLOCAUST

that said they weren't Jewish, but the Gestapo caught me with the papers. I was interrogated and beaten badly. I was lucky a major stopped the beating, because how could I tell them the papers were for my mother and sister?

"They transported me to the jail of the Plaschau labor camp on Jerusalemskaya Street, in a suburb of Cracow. In jail they came in every few days and took out thirty or forty to be shot, but I was lucky. I got out of jail because a friend of my father was in charge of the horses and wagons at the labor camp, and he told me to say I knew how to shoe horses.

"There had been a Jewish cemetery on Jerusalemskaya, hundreds of years old, but the Germans took away the tombstones. Now it was just barracks, about 800 Jews in a work camp. Most worked in agriculture or went to factories in the city. A small number were mechanics, machinists, welders.

"Then the Germans liquidated the ghettoes in southern Poland, and in three months the camp grew to about 35,000. Then they brought in Dutch, Germans, Belgians, and the camp population swelled to about 70,000. At 5 a.m., they made Jewish musicians play reveille on the trumpet to wake us. Then we had some bread or a little soup. We were hungry all the time, and always there was fear. The guards were Volksdeutch from Poland, Romania, Hungary, Yugoslavia, the Ukraine. They lived outside the camp, unscrupulous beasts in black uniforms. The camp commander, Amnon Goeth, was born in Vienna, appreciated art and music, and had a Jewish orchestra. If he saw a man hitting an unruly horse, he would shoot the man on the spot or tell his two Dalmatian dogs, 'Get him,' and they would tear the man apart.

"Every day we saw people shot, torn by dogs. Nobody knew if their last minute was approaching. It was hell. In January 1945 the Russians were near, so we were put in buggies and taken west about thirty miles to Auschwitz. With the Russians approaching, we were then transported to Buchenwald. From there we marched to Flossenburg. Hundreds died on those marches.

"The Americans were approaching Flossenburg, so we were marched to Dachau. It was dark, raining. I saw my chance and ran into the woods. I came to a farm and climbed on top of the wooden silo, very high. I hid there for four days, eating corn and grain. Then American tanks came rolling by! There were Jewish soldiers, American Jews, and I could talk to them in Yiddish. They took me to Floss, a little village nearby, where there were maybe a thousand Jews who had been marching to Dachau. They put us with German families and told them to give us food.

"This was April 1945 and the war ended May 8. In June I found my younger brother in Waldenburg, Germany. I got news that my sister survived Bergen-Belsen, and we went there and got her. My father had been sent to Grossrosen, so we went there but couldn't find any sign of him. He'd been 'liquidated.' My older brother, too. Then I heard my mother and my other sister were in Cracow, 700 miles away. I stole a motorcycle. Along the way I asked a Russian soldier if there was a place I could stay overnight. He and his friends took my motorcycle and threw me in a cellar. They locked me in there for two days. Then they took me to their headquarters, guns cocked. Luckily there was a Jewish officer there, a Russian Jew, who set me free, but he didn't want to give the motorcycle up, so I walked and went by train to Cracow.

"I decided to take my family to Bavaria, in the American zone. We traveled by train, in open boxcars. You didn't even buy tickets, you just got on, and nobody checked. The bridges were destroyed, so a trip that would normally take one day took ten days.

"In Feldafing, Germany, a displaced persons camp, the refugee committee gave us food and clothing. The beginning of 1946 I moved to Munzberg, where I had some friends. I didn't want to live anymore in camps, didn't want anybody giving me welfare. A friend and I established a company, buying steel from the mills, selling to hardware stores and builders. In 1948 I registered to go to the U.S. I was 'processed' with photos, X-rays, hundreds of questions. Some government officials seemed anti-Jewish, especially people from the state department. Finally we sailed for America on an old military ship.

"It's unbelievable to be a survivor of the Holocaust. Films, books, nothing can describe it. There were a lot of people more capable, more deserving than I to survive, but I had the right profession, so I survived and they did not."

MAX GOODMAN

RADAUTI, ROMANIA

"There was a river nearby and people used to go very early in the morning to take baths. The river was outside the ghetto and people were killed there if they were caught. Killed because they went to take a bath!"

Although his Hasidic ancestors had come to Radauti in 1718, Max Goodman's family was still considered "foreign" because they were Jews. His father was a grain merchant and dealer in agricultural products. Max was sixteen when the war began.

"We were friendly with our gentile neighbors, but separate, never close," said Max. "In school Jewish students were always apart. Already in the 1930s the trend was more and more to blame the Jews for everything wrong in the Romania. They wanted the Jews to leave the country. Radauti was close to the Polish border. After war broke out in Poland, refugees came into Romania. A committee of citizens went house to house and asked who would accept Polish people for a short stay. We had a big house, so two Polish army officers came to our house, but when they saw the mezuzah on the door they refused to come in.

"By 1940 part of Romania was occupied by Russia, and the Jews were blamed for betraying Romania. At that time we had Jewish refugees staying in our home because all the Jews in villages were fleeing to the cities.

"Life carried on, with new anti-Jewish regulations every day. Romanian police would take a hundred Jews and keep them in custody 'just in case.' They said if Jews attacked gentiles, hostages would be executed. The police came to my home and arrested me, but they'd change hostages maybe every two weeks, so I came home okay. Then my father was thrown from a moving train by the Iron Guard, and six months later he died.

"In 1941 the Germans' attacked Russia, with Romania a full-fledged ally of the Berlin-Rome axis. In October 1941 it was announced in the newspaper that all Jews in Radauti had to present themselves at the railroad station to be resettled in the 'territories of the east,' where Romania had occupied part of Russia. My grandparents, my mother, my sister and I were deported, taking just what we could carry on our backs. We were pushed into cattle wagons and traveled a couple of days into Transnistria, then by foot about fifty miles.

"In Dzurin, for sixteen people we had a room about eight by ten feet, a kitchen about half that size, and another little room. A sack with some straw was my bed for three-and-a-half years. There was a ten-bed hospital

Max Goodman with father

with Jewish doctors, but they used to keep 100 people there. We almost all had typhoid fever and most of the doctors died taking care of sick people.

"In that whole city of 4,000 there was just one water pump. I was so thirsty I drank muddy water from the river. From this I got dysentery, and I got so weak I couldn't even move from my bed. Then a relative came with some brandy made out of sugar beets, hot barley bread, and pieces of fried animal fat, and after two or three days I got better. I found work in a slaughterhouse, so our family had meat. In the morning when we used to open the doors to clean, we would throw out little pieces of meat, bone, skin, and 200 or 300 people would fight over these remnants.

"Once a week, for two hours, Jews were allowed into an open marketplace to barter with peasants—bread in exchange for a pair of socks, fifty pounds of flour for a suit. Of 200,000 Jews deported into Transnistria in 1941, 150,000 died of starvation by 1943. In the morning you would see people lying in the street who had died overnight. A pushcart used to pick up these people and take them to their graves.

"In 1944 we began to see German troops retreating, going west day and night. Suddenly in March there were no more Germans, and then the Russians came in. A Jewish captain in the Russian army came with the first Russians into our ghetto and found his father there!

"The population when we got home was very friendly. Romania formed a democratic government in 1945, and there was freedom. Then in 1948 the Communists came to power. The Communists introduced identity cards and we had to declare our nationality. We could have said, 'Okay, I'm not a Jew anymore. I see myself now as a Romanian national.' But most of Romania's Jews didn't change.

"I went to school and started earning some money, so I could leave. But in 1951, when we thought maybe it was time to go, they began closing and opening the borders, back and forth. In some cities they would give permits, in some they wouldn't. I didn't get my exit papers until 1958—seven years!"

MAX GROSBLAT

DUBNO, POLAND

"I was nineteen when the Germans came. I wanted to get out but there was no place to go. Then I stole two rifles and joined the partisans. Not all the Jewish people went to death like sheep. Some of us were fighting!"

Max Grosblat was the son of deeply religious Jews and thought about becoming a rabbi, or a cantor. Instead, he became "Fearless Mischka" of the partisans.

"My ancestors came from Germany and settled in Poland during the Crusades," said Max. "Dubno was in the Polish Ukraine, famous for its apple and pear orchards, a lot of poultry, eggs. It was a town of about 70,000 people, 10,000 Jewish. Everybody Jewish spoke Yiddish, Hebrew, and Polish. I also spoke Ukrainian.

"My dad was a tailor and spoke to his customers in their own languages—German, Ukrainian, Polish, Russian and Czech. He'd take their size and make a suit from scratch. Some didn't have money to pay so they traded farm products for their clothes. Most of our customers were gentiles. We did not talk politics with them; we talked about a suit or pants or a jacket. We also knew we had to stay away from the church after Sunday services because when they came out they looked for Jews to start a fight. But my friends and I were a bunch of tough Jewish guys who never stepped away from a fight.

"I was seventeen when the war started and the Russians took our part of Poland. Polish citizens expelled from Germany came to our town and told us the Germans had destroyed Jewish businesses and broken windows, but we didn't hear of anybody getting killed. When the Germans came in on June 24, 1941, right away they ordered all Jewish people to move south of the city, near the river. They gave us an area about three blocks wide from north to south, and seven blocks long from east to west. We were already living where the ghetto was, but now there were three families in our four-room house. I was working for the police, cutting wood, but we didn't have enough to heat the house, so I was breaking up fences to bring wood home, and my family was selling whatever we could to get food.

"Then the ghetto was divided. My father didn't work, so they told us to move to the other side of the ghetto. The guy I worked for couldn't tell me that if you move to the side with the ones who didn't work, you wouldn't live long, but he said, 'You should stay where you are,' so we did. Three months later, they took those families on the other side out of the city about five kilometers—3,000 people—and shot them!

"I was working in a garage where on one side we were sawing wood, and on the other side police were collecting weapons the Russians threw away as they fled the German army. I took two rifles, a long one and a cut-off short one. I had a two-wheeler to take sawdust home, so I put the two rifles in the bottom, put some rags around, filled it up with sawdust, and wheeled it home. I dug out a place and hid the rifles, but some people saw me, other Jews. Word got around and someone told me, 'We're organizing. Get in touch if you want to join.'

"Then a lot of Ukrainian policemen and S.S. came into town, and we decided it was time to leave. On the other side of town was a factory making sausages, and Jewish people used to work there. We lined up in a group, with

Jewish policemen escorting us through the town, as if they were marching us to work. Then, when we should have turned right to the factory, we turned left and kept marching! That was October 3. On October 5 they liquidated the ghetto.

"We were a group of fifty, mostly young guys of nineteen or twenty. A Ukrainian took my rifles out of the ghetto to the woods, which were divided into sections, and we were assigned Section 15. I was told I would get my rifles back there, but when we came into the woods, nobody could tell us where section 15 was! So we were just a group of people without a leader, without contacts, without weapons, without anything. Some of the people had gold pieces, and we would go to villages to buy food, or go out into the fields and take potatoes or cabbage or carrots.

"At that time a man could get two pounds of sugar if he found a Jew, and someone showed the Germans where we were. Some of us had gone to dig a winter shelter, and we heard shots and came back and found two of our people dead. We decided to leave that area, but first I went to the village and I told a peasant about my two rifles. He told me that the man I gave the rifles to was in the other room! So I got back my sawed-off shotgun and some bullets. I got my rifle back.

Max Grosblat

"Ukrainians were trying to steal whatever they could and were giving the Polish population trouble, so we guarded the Polish people in these villages and stayed in their houses. Word got around to Russian partisans that there was a Jewish group with weapons, so the Russians came to us to ask if we wanted to join them as partisans.

"There were very few Jews in the partisans, and the other partisans hated us. One fellow went to see his mother, and Ukrainians took his rifle away. When he came back without the rifle, his own comrades locked him in a barn and burned the barn! Another Jewish fellow didn't want to admit he was Jewish. They played a Jewish tune on the record player, and he was humming the tune, so they shot him.

"I almost got killed, too. They gave me horses to take care of, and I didn't know to put ropes on their front feet so they wouldn't escape. I just put them in the pasture, and when we were supposed to start out, the horses were gone! But one fellow knew me from before the war and he told them, 'He's a businessman. What does he know about horses?' That saved me.

"When I joined the partisans in February 1943, there were about 200 people in that partisan group. By April 1944, there were 2,000, and I was part of the general staff. They knew they could depend on me because I was not afraid. I didn't care if I got killed. I was there to kill as many Germans as I could, to take revenge.

"We blew up bridges, and when German trains were going to the front with ammunition and weapons, we put dynamite under the tracks. You had to hide and pull a string to ignite it. Nobody wanted that dangerous job, so I did it. And when they wanted to find out if Germans were in an area, they would send me out on reconnaissance. They called me Mischka the Fearless.

"For supplies we had an airfield. At night we used to make fires on four corners of the field, and planes would come down and bring automatic weapons, explosives, things like that. We were in contact with Moscow by radio. When the war ended we hitchhiked home. Back home there was nothing. Our house was demolished, rubble. I was the oldest of five children, and the only one left was my sister. My mother and father, three brothers, uncles, aunts, cousins—there was nobody left. Across the street we had Polish friends, gentiles, and I stayed with them. I found out my father lived in hiding about three months after the liquidation. Then he went to peasants he used to know in a village, but he didn't make it.

"Not all Germans were murderers. One I worked for used to bring me a loaf of bread hidden in his uniform. And there was one German-Austrian who took a risk and warned the Jews before the liquidation. He drove in the streets of the ghetto on his motorcycle and hollered, 'This is going to be the end of you! Jews, get out!'

"I met my wife in the partisans. We got married July 12, 1945, and in December we came to Berlin and then to a displaced persons camp in the American zone. I took up auto mechanics and they offered me a job as an instructor. We had one room, with a kitchen set up in the bathroom. If somebody had to go to the bathroom you had to leave your cooking! Three years we lived like that. We came to the United States in 1949.

"I had a feeling even as a kid that I had to fight for my rights, to fight when nobody else would. You must fight for what you believe in."

EDWARD GROSMANN

MEDZILABORCE, CZECHOSLOVAKIA

"The kapo said, 'Listen, I'm a brother of yours, a Czech. I'm here because I was a Communist. In the presence of the S.S. I'll yell, I'll kick, I'll beat the living hell out of you. Otherwise I'll leave you in peace.' I survived because of him."

Edward Grosmann began Hebrew school at age three, finished his secular education at fourteen, but continued his Jewish studies until the Nazis took over Czechoslovakia. He was seventeen years old when the war began.

"My ancestors were farmers even before the Jews were allowed to hold land," said Ed. "Legend goes that they had settled in Medzilaborce many centuries before, that they may have been refugees from the Spanish Inquisition. My father was already in the United States. He had come back to Czechoslovakia in 1919, and left again in 1925. My mother stayed and carried on in a very small general store.

"In Medzilaborce 70 percent of the townspeople were Jews. I had non-Jewish friends and I never felt any anti-Semitism, but we realized, for example, that most of us would not have a chance to go to the university because there was a secret quota system and only so many Jews were able to attend. I was very active in our small business, and most of our customers were non-Jews from outlying areas. Later some of them even tried to hide my sister during the deportations.

"We had a very small group of Zionists, continuously fighting with the elders of our Jewish community, who could not see the need for a Jewish state in Palestine. Their very traditional approach was that only when God decides that the Messiah should come and redeem His people will be time to go. When we saw the fall of Austria in 1938, I tried to escape to Palestine. But Slovakia declared independence from Czechoslovakia and became an ally of Nazi Germany, Hitler marched into Prague, and it was too late.

"Our neighbors became the Nazis. They immediately forced us to wear yellow stars. I was kicked out of school, and our non-Jewish friends stayed away from us because associating with Jews was punishable by imprisonment. The regime took over our little business, kicked us out, and gave the business to non-Jews.

Edward Grosmann (left)

"All the young Jews were taken away from their homes and families and had to do public labor—cleaning streets, helping build roads. We were not paid and had to provide our own food. There was a great celebration in Slovakia when Hitler marched into Poland. We Jews, meanwhile, could not believe the things we had been hearing on BBC about Germany and Austria

73

taking Jews to prison and torturing them, but we were afraid and very worried. Then some relatives came from Poland and told us about the Nazis taking people out into the streets and murdering them in cold blood, and about the ghettoes. We heard a big ghetto was being created near Prague, called Terezin, and that many Jews were being taken away to the east for labor. We went to the synagogue and prayed for God to save us.

"In 1941, I was drafted into the Slovak army, just like the non-Jews. I went through basic training like all the other soldiers, except we used a shovel instead of a gun. Then we were sent into labor battalions in uniform, to build roads, railroads, and other war-important projects. There were over 2,500 of us in Jewish battalions. There was no persecution, other than we were wearing a blue uniform instead of a green uniform. Gypsies wore a brown uniform.

"Our living conditions were as good as any other soldier's. We were allowed to worship in our barracks any way we chose, and on Jewish holidays we could arrange with the supervisors to make up our quota of time during the evening or on Sunday. We got the same pay, the same food, and it was agreed that we would not have to accept non-kosher food. There was no kosher meat available, but we were able to get beans and peas and bread, which made up in dollars and cents the money allocated to feed us. By then, our families were gone, and we were the only Jews left in Czechoslovakia, 2,500 out of maybe 100,000.

"After the war we learned the Slovak minister of defense knew what was going on in Poland and he felt that at least he could save some of us. In July 1943, however, the Nazis pressured the Slovak army and we Jews were all discharged. We returned the uniforms and the army supervisors left, but 410 of us stayed in our barracks at the brick factory, performing the same labor.

"Our gentile coworkers would hear rumors that the S.S. was coming to pick us up, so we'd run off to the woods and hide. Then our gentile coworkers would come tell us it seems like everything is quiet, so we'd come back. This went on for sixteen or seventeen months. Then on October 28, 1944, several thousand S.S. with machine guns and cannons came to capture the 410 of us! They handcuffed us and threw us into trucks, five or six of us in one truck with ten or fifteen S.S. men!

"We arrived in Auschwitz November 1, 1944. We were the last transport to Auschwitz. We saw the chimneys and smelled the smell of burning flesh, and we knew what was going on because some people who had come back from Majdanek had told us that there would be a selection, and all the children and older people would be killed on the spot. So we were very surprised that, though we saw the big dogs and heard the yelling, they didn't divide us up.

"We waited two weeks. Then they lined us up, men to the right, women separately, children separately. 'This is it,' we thought. We went through the shower, and again we were afraid because we had heard about those so-called showers. Then we got uniforms. Two Jewish boys started giving us tattoos, these numbers, and they were doing the same thing with the women and children. We were no longer people, we were numbers. I was B14083.

"We were sent to dig rutabagas. The mud was up to our knees, and we knew we wouldn't last long. Then a kapo came to the barracks, a political prisoner with the red triangle on his uniform, and he wanted twenty Czechs. We had a conference. Should we dare volunteer? We decided we didn't have much to lose so we volunteered.

"We didn't know what was going to happen, but at five the next morning, the kapo and the S.S. picked us up and took us to the weaving factory, only about 100 steps away! There was an enormous warehouse full of pieces of plastic, and we were to distribute it to women who would weave it into ropes for the German navy. These women had lost the look of human beings. Such people were called 'musselmen.' They were human skeletons.

"The S.S. left. Our kapo was named Gottfried. I can see his face as if it was today. It was a very cold winter, but I survived because I worked inside that factory and because of him.

"January 18 was the evacuation of Auschwitz. We were about 30,000 people marching to Gliwice. It was snowing bitterly. It was maybe sixty miles and it took three days. People were so tired or sick they would just sit down, and the S.S. would push them into ditches and kill them. More than half the people in our group didn't make it to Gliwice. After two days in Gliwice, they told all the Jews to come out. I didn't try to hide because I looked Jewish. Some Jews, blonds who didn't look Jewish, did try to hide but the evil Polish prisoners, they called out to the S.S., 'Here's a Jew!'

"We wound up on a big train in open cars, about 200 per car. There was hardly room to breathe! They gave a bread to each prisoner. We traveled

75

seven days, all over Poland, Czechoslovakia. Half the people in our car died, and we had to throw them out of the car when the train stopped. In Czechoslovakia people saw the cars going by and some threw us bread. We were scrambling like mad dogs, so hungry that some people killed each other for a piece of bread!

"We came to Mauthausen, but we were not allowed to get out because there was no more room in the camp. It took another seven days to come to Sachsenhausen. There was no food for those seven days. The only thing we had was the snow coming into our train, except at Oranienburg, where we got some hot water, the first time we had anything in our mouths from the Germans in fourteen days.

"There were thirty of us left alive, from a car of at least 200. I was very, very hungry, very sick. After three or four days, we were divided into groups to go to work camps. I was sent to Flossenburg, to the stone quarries, but we were so weak we could no longer lift even a little stone! People were dying very quickly because we all got dysentery. They put six people in a bunk, and every morning there were one or two dead.

"Then they sent us to a place where supposedly we were going to build an airfield. We were as capable of building airfields as I am capable of walking to the moon. But we went to the airport, about 300 of us. We built tents and we slept there. We supposedly were pouring cement, but we couldn't do much of anything. Every day people died or were killed because they weren't moving fast enough.

"Then, the American air force started dropping bombs so they marched us out again. Anybody who slowed down was shot. And then, on a Friday afternoon, April 27, we were not far from Dachau, and an S.S. man read a message: 'All prisoners are now free, and should report to the American army.' It was a sunny day. The wildflowers and the daffodils were out, and it was very bright. There was no jubilation because people were so weak that many of them just didn't have the strength to get up. But a few of us picked ourselves up. Instinct told us, 'Move. Try to see what it feels like to be free.'

"Two other fellows and I walked slowly into the neighboring town in our striped, filthy prisoners' uniforms. A farmer told us we could rest in the haystack and brought us some boiled potatoes. We stole eggs and ate them raw.

"The next morning the farmer told us the S.S. had been there asking for prisoners. He told us he would bring us food, but in case we were caught, not to say he'd been helping us.

"We were in that haystack until May 2 when we saw tanks. Americans! They threw us chocolate and took us into town. We broke into a bakery where the bread was still half raw, but we started eating. I wound up in a hospital unconscious. I was in the hospital for about two-and-a-half months, very sick. American doctors brought me back to life. I remembered the address of my brother in the United States. The day his first letter came, that's when I really woke up from that nightmare.

"The Czech government sent trucks to bring us back home, and we came back as national heroes. There wasn't much housing or food, but the government gave us housing and double rations. We got free schooling and jobs, free tickets to all the theaters and to the symphony. I found one survivor from the transport my mother and sister were on. She told me my mother was murdered by a drunken S.S. man, one sister vanished in Majdanek, one in Treblinka. My whole family was gone, at least 150 aunts, uncles, cousins. There wasn't a single survivor.

"I saw the Communists taking over the country, and rumors were that there would be a coup. I was working for the trade ministry and arranged to go to Canada in December 1947, to represent the Czech textile industry. I never went back. My brother got me a visa and I came to Minneapolis. I tried to get a job in international trade. I went to all the big companies that had an international department—Cargill, 3M, General Mills, Pillsbury, Honeywell. Everybody was very nice. 'Mr. Grosmann, it's wonderful to meet you. We'll call you.' But nobody called. Then I went to an employment agency and they told me, 'There isn't a single Jew working in those companies. You'll never get a job there.' But eventually I met the president of a company who gave me an opportunity and I became a senior vice president. America has been good to me.

"I was brought up in a very religious home in a very religious community. I believed very strongly in God. In Auschwitz, I lost total belief in any supreme being. I didn't want to have anything to do with the God who let my little nephew be burned alive in Auschwitz. When I met my future wife, I told her I wanted to get married by a justice of the peace. She said, 'No synagogue, no wedding.' Before I knew it, I was woven into the fabric of religious and community life, and I don't regret it.

"The most important thing to me, as a survivor, is the price I have paid to be a Jew. In the last moments of the war, when I weighed only eighty pounds and was very ill, what kept me going was that I wanted to see the downfall of the Nazi regime, to see the Jewish people survive. And I did."

EVA GROSS AND ELLA WEISS

HUNGARY

"I took my father's name and my mother took her maiden name. That way we were registered, we were no relation to each other."

Eva Gross and her mother Ella Weiss

The story of Eva Gross and her mother Ella Weiss is a tale of devotion of a mother and daughter who together survived deportation from their small Hungarian village, six concentration camps including Auschwitz, forced labor, death marches and finally liberation.

Eva was sixteen years old when, said Eva, "We got the knock on the door and the Hungarian police came. They said, 'You people have to take a suitcase with a few personal things and come with us.' So we had to go— my mother, my grandmother, my grandfather and myself, four of us. My father had

78

been taken away before." Eva's grandfather was a religious man and she knew that his tallit (prayer shawl), which he used daily, would certainly be among the most important items to pack. When she saw that it wasn't packed, she was puzzled. "Mein kind (my child)," she remembered him saying, "where we are going, I won't need it." He had a premonition of what was to come.

With their belongings, said Eva, "we were herded into the synagogue, everybody from the town. I don't remember how long we spent in the synagogue but then we were taken to the state capital." The police, under Nazi supervision, were rounding up all Jewish residents of rural Hungary for deportation. The first stop was a makeshift ghetto in the regional capital where all Jews from the area were detained. "Then the Hungarian army came and lined us up and told us that we were going to be taken someplace where we could set up a home, find a job and settle in. They lined us up, took us into the railroad station. There was an engine with I don't know how many cattle cars." The Hungarians turned the Jews over to Nazi officials and they were herded onto cattle cars bound for Auschwitz.

"They pushed as many people as possible into these cattle cars. My mother, my grandmother and I were pushed into one and for some reason my grandfather didn't make it. So he got into another one. There wasn't enough room for everybody to sit down. So one person was sitting and one was standing. Then we changed around to give everybody and ourselves a chance to relax a bit. And in the middle of the car they had a huge, huge pail with a cover and if you had to go to the bathroom you had to relieve yourself right there and then in front of everybody. There was no cover. There was nothing. Somebody had a blanket so we used it to give people privacy. There was no water and no food. The smell and the air in the train were beyond description. One person died and the body was there traveling with us.

"When the doors of the train opened at Auschwitz, the S.S. kept on yelling 'fast, fast.' They wanted us to go faster. So people were practically tumbling out of the train. Then they had a 'selection.'" The young people capable of working were sent to the right but those deemed unfit for labor were sent to the left. Eva remembered that her mother immediately noticed that her grandparents were being taken to a truck. "I better go see grandma and grandpa and help them," said Eva's mother. Ella Weiss attempted to join her parents but an S.S. guard grabbed her and threw her back in line with her daughter. "I said to my mom, 'Don't do that, you don't know what's happening. Let's stay here.' As it turned out, this S.S. man saved her life because the people on the truck were immediately taken to the gas chamber."

One of the inmates assigned to work at the train station told Eva's mother that if they were a family with the same name they should give different last names to the S.S. because families were automatically separated. "I took my father's name and my mother took her maiden name. That way we were registered, we were no relation to each other."

"Following the selection, the prisoners were assigned to barracks and given a food ration, which consisted of a piece of bread and a bowl of soup. I ate the soup and I was allergic to it, so I broke into a rash. So my mother said, 'You take the bread and I'll take the soup,' and we divided it. My mother and I made up our minds that whatever had to be done, we would do to survive."

They protected each other through stays in six concentration camps. When guard dogs attacked Ella for using the latrine, Eva bandaged her leg with scraps of cloth torn from her dress so the guards wouldn't discover her injury. When Eva had trouble using the sewing machines in the factory where they worked, Eva did both jobs so that Ella wouldn't be sent away.

In the winter of 1945 they were sent on a forced march to Bergen-Belsen. With no coats or shoes many people died of starvation and exposure. Ella gave up hope; she grew weak and thought she couldn't go on. She said to her daughter, "I have to let them kill me and this will be the end of my life." Eva continued, "We were walking and an S.S. man—I don't know if his conscience was bothering him or if he was afraid because he knew the war was coming to an end—but he came to us. He told us to drag my mother, that we were almost there." Eva and Ella made it to Bergen-Belsen where they were liberated by the British.

Ella died in 2011 at the age of 101. Eva continues to tell her story to school groups.

CHARLOTTE HIRSCH

TRANSYLVANIA

"On Shabbat, the guards beat us more, gave us more work. On Yom Kippur we were taken a long way to work and came back to camp after dark, and our food was much worse than other days because they knew it was Yom Kippur."

Charlotte Czitron was eighteen when World War II began. Her father managed forests for a lumber company, and she grew up in a warm, loving family with lots of laughter. At Auschwitz Dr. Mengele selected Charlotte for life but sent her mother and father to the gas chamber.

"I came from a very religious family," said Charlotte, "not rich, not poor. We had nice dresses and a nice education. My father was tall, very good-looking and a very good man. My mother always said she never wanted to survive one minute without my father. They died together in Auschwitz.

"My father used to go to the synagogue every evening, and one day he came home and said, 'Something very wrong is coming. There is a Polish Jew here who is saying we'll be taken to a ghetto where terrible things happen and they kill people.' My mother said, 'I don't want to hear about it.'

"When the Germans arrived, we were ordered to wear yellow stars. The Germans took all the Jews out of a large fancy apartment building, They stole Oriental rugs and silver and crystal. Jewish girls had to clean the apartments, and some of the German soldiers who supervised, would rape some of the girls and threaten, 'If you say one word, I will kill all your family.' We were so afraid.

"My brother went into the Hungarian army in 1940, but after a couple of months he was transferred to the work battalion. My other brother went to the work battalion, too. I was working as a dressmaker. But then Jews were forbidden to work. Bucharest was under bombardment, but my sister who lived there was risking her life going to the railroad station to send us packages of silk stockings and other things we could sell to buy food. Then they stopped letting Jews go to the market. They took our bicycles, the radio, cars, everything. Then there was a knock on our door, and soldiers saying, 'You have a sewing machine,' and they took it.

"One day our neighbor said, 'Tomorrow morning we're going to be taken away.' My mother said to me, 'Go to sleep and don't think about tomorrow.' We were so close to the border that if you walked just one hour you'd be in Romania. In twelve hours we could have been in Bucharest with my sister. But my father said, 'I'm not going. I don't want to be separate from my neighbors. Whatever happens to everybody else will happen to me.'

"The morning of May 3 my mother was preparing lamb for dinner and a neighbor came running and said, 'Come look, come to the gate.' I saw a long line of people with packages on their backs, in their hands. So we quickly packed what we could, clothes, feather comforters, pillows, cooking pots. The Hungarian police—they wore rooster feathers in their hats! —came to take us to the brick burner outside town. The lamb was left cooking on the stove.

"At the brick burner there was a basket. We had to put in our wedding rings. All our other jewelry had already been taken. It wasn't really a building, only four posts and a leaky roof, rocks and dogs' dirt. It was raining. We put down our comforter in that dirty place and tried to sleep.

"We couldn't wash regularly. There was no medicine, no food. People who had more food shared with others and everybody gave food to the children. Our nanny from when I was a child tried to bring us food, but it never got through to us.

"On May 29 we were taken to the railroad station. The street was silent, nobody outside, but we saw people looking out their windows at us, curious to see what was going on. We stood in line for a whole day —old people, young, sick, pregnant, everybody crying. People almost couldn't walk because they were carrying so many packages. It was so hot people were fainting, and we couldn't help because we couldn't move out of the line. My father was like a statue, so tall and strong and very proud.

"We were put in railroad cars, eighty people to a car. The Germans pushed and beat us. We had no food, no water. That was Thursday. On Friday my mother started to cry because she couldn't light Shabbat candles. Sunday morning we arrived in Auschwitz. It was dark and foggy. The train car was very high up off the ground, and they beat us when we jumped down. We saw an officer, very tall, very good-looking, very imposing. I now know his name was Mengele because I talked to him when I tried to save my mother.

"Mengele said, 'Right, left.' My father could not go to the right because he had lost his hand, a war injury. My mother was very pretty, and I put my red scarf on my mother's head so she would look young. But Mengele put his stick between us and sent her to the left. When he turned away I went to my mother, but he took me back to the right side. Somebody said, 'Look, there are the children, the babies.' Very far away we saw silhouettes of women pushing baby carriages, but later we found out there were no babies in the carriages. The carriages were full of valuables being sent to Germany.

"An S.S. woman said to us, 'Take off everything.' I think of my mother with all these strange people naked, and the German soldiers watching, and I cry. I had long, black, beautiful hair and they cut it off. Then into the showers, many under one shower, very little water, and so cold. Everything happened so fast, no dress, no hair, no nothing, wet and cold like an animal. I got a red and white silk dress that was short and very thin. I picked up two shoes, both for the same foot, one with a high heel and the other one flat. In August, like a miracle, another prisoner gave me a dress with long sleeves and a high collar. Otherwise I would have died from the cold.

"I was three months in Auschwitz. We had one meal in the morning after rollcall—a piece of old bread, a bit of marmalade, sometimes a piece of cheese crawling with worms, and coffee-colored liquid. We went to work digging trenches in the forest. My feet were freezing. I was beaten, my nose broken, with broken ribs and a lung hemorrhage. Then we were taken to Stutthof for the gas chamber. But there were too many before us, and they had no more gas, so we escaped death. From Stutthof I was taken to Bromberg, where I became a tailor for the S.S.

"In January 1945 the Russians were coming, so the Germans marched us out. We walked for seven days. The road was slippery, the S.S. were shooting people, and all the time there were bombings. And then one morning we got up and there were no Germans. The war was over for us.

"Three of us, three girls, travelled January and February, until the end of March. Russian Jewish soldiers gave us food, but they could not give us rides because it was still the war there. We walked to Lublin, and after Lublin we found a train and traveled across Warsaw.

"Six months before then, my town had been freed, and my brothers were back. I was sick with headaches and pain. I didn't want to believe my parents wouldn't come back. I went to Bucharest to live with my sister and brother-in-law. I became elegant again, and I learned to live with the pain. I knew Alexander Hirsch from before the war, from the Zionist youth group Hashomer Hatzair. We had dated for six years before the war. When I got home somebody said to me, 'You don't have to wait for him. He had typhus and he must have died.' But after a couple of months in Bucharest, I felt like I had to go back to my hometown. Alex was there, and we got married. We first went to Palestine, and in 1968 we came to the United States. Three times I stood in front of the gas chamber and lived. Not many can say this."

CURT HORT

BERLIN, GERMANY

"'We'll give you another thirty minutes,' said the Japanese. 'Then, we will pick twenty-five pregnant women and kill them in front of you'—which they did with bayonets—I'll never forget that in my life."

Curt Hort was seventeen years old when life in Germany became so threatening for Jews that his mother made the decision to take the only escape route available to the family and flee to Shanghai, China. Embassies all over the world were closing their doors, including the United States. But there was one place that Jews could go which didn't require a visa for entry—Shanghai.

Curt remembers that and his family lived a middle-class. life in suburban Berlin. Life began to change with the Nazis' rise to power in the early 1930's. Curt was one of only two Jewish students at a top Berlin elementary school when another student, a member of the Hitler Youth, threw him down the school steps. Shortly after that incident, both Jewish students were dismissed from the school. "We were kicked out because we couldn't meet the requirements. They screamed 'Jews out!' And two little boys went out, we had to leave the school."

In 1939 during Kristallnacht, Curt's father was taken to a concentration camp. "My mother had bought tickets to Shanghai and she went to the Commandant and asked him to release my father." Miraculously, Curt's father was released and a "few months later we went to Shanghai. It took us about four weeks from leaving Italy on the boat."

Following the Battle of Shanghai in 1937, the Army of Imperial Japan occupied the city. Between 1938 and 1941, thousands of refugees found temporary refuge in the Japanese-occupied city of Shanghai. "It had an international concession, which was run mostly by American and English," said Curt. "The Dutch shared a certain part of it and the French had their own concession. It was a foreign island in a city of a few million people."

"When we came to Shanghai, it was a miserable town of crime, prostitution, dope and dirt." The Jews were settled in the poorest part of the city, the impoverished Hongkew District. The Hort family was assigned to the Choufoong Hou Heim refugee camp. "We were put into an area of Shanghai that was greatly demolished during the Chinese-Japanese war. The refugee camp was an old school for deaf children. We had two toilets for 100 people—men, women, and children."

Despite aid from an international committee, remembers Curt, living conditions were brutal, with crowded shabby apartments, meager food rations and little or no sanitation. "The food was awful. It was hardboiled eggs laid by chickens who were fed fish, and the eggs exploded with fish smell."

"After the war started, the Japanese took over Shanghai and that is when it really got bad.when it really got bad," said Curt. "The Japanese occupiers were brutal. One incident explainsit. Toward the end of the war, a Japanese officer's army car was blown up by the Chinese underground in an area in Hongkew which was the lowest part of Shanghai. The Japanese ordered a round-up of all the residents of the area; thousands of Chinese and Jewish refugees were corralled into a barbed-wire playground. The Japanese demanded illogically that the poor, innocent people give the names of the people who bombed the officer's car. Nobody knew, of course! Who knows what the Underground does? Standing in the sun, a lot of people tipped over, lost consciousness. Then they came out and said, 'We'll give you another thirty minutes. Then, we will pick twenty-five pregnant women and kill them in front of you'—which they did with bayonets—I'll never forget that in my life."

"The Japanese had a pact with the Nazis and the Italians. The Nazis pressured the Japanese general to have the Jews in Shanghai gassed. S.S. Colonel Meisinger, who was known as the Butcher of Warsaw, was sent to Shanghai to build gas chambers. We were very close to being pushed into a gas chamber when the A bomb fell on Hiroshima."

The bombing of Hiroshima saved the Hort family along with the other Jews of the Shanghai Ghetto. The Horts left Shanghai in 1947 for San Francisco feeling "free and grateful."

FELIX KAMINSKY

SENDJESZOW, POLAND

"'Can you imagine being one of eight children and not having anybody left in the world?' I asked the rabbi, 'If there's a God, why didn't He send a miracle? Why was He waiting while 6,000,000 Jews were killed?' There is no answer."

Felix Kaminsky wanted to emigrate to Palestine but was drafted into the Polish army in 1936. During the war, he did slave labor at the airport near Cracow until he was assigned to work for Oskar Schindler.

"One-third of Sendjeszow was Jewish, about 100 families," said Felix. "Even when I was a small boy, there was anti-Semitism. Before Easter the gentiles used to throw things at us. When we became army recruits, Jewish boys used to have the best scores on tests, but the captain said to us, 'I'm not able to send you to officers' school.' Why? Because we were Jews.

"I was in Hashomer Hatzair, a Zionist youth movement, and went on *hachsherah* (agricultural training) so I could go to Palestine. But in 1936 I was drafted into the Polish army for eighteen months, and when I came back, my group was gone. They had all immigrated to Palestine. I went back in the army in 1939, fighting against Hitler. I was a special shooter on the front line, with a hundred-pound pack on my shoulders and a big gun. When we lost, the captain told us we should all get home on our own. A Polish friend and I took two horses and a buggy, and a priest gave us two old priests' robes to use as disguises. We found a barn to sleep in, but it was freezing, and the farmer told us to come into the kitchen. While we were asleep he stole our horses, so we traveled the 200 miles by train to get home.

"The Germans organized a Judenrat in the ghetto, a Jewish council that would be responsible for us going to work every morning. Women and young girls they took to Cracow to work at the airport. I worked on railroad tracks cutting steel wires. One day the German guard was playing around spinning a wire around his head, and it went into my eye. A Jewish policeman took me to the hospital, where two Jewish doctors took out my eye. I used to wear a black patch.

"At the first selection, in 1941, I took a handkerchief and started wiping my eye, as if maybe something was in it, so they wouldn't see the eyepatch. The Germans put the young, healthy people on wagons. Then they told the old people to run, and they shot them in the back—my family, the rabbi, over a hundred people. Polish farmers came with wagons and buried the dead in the forest.

"My niece worked for a German guy at the airport in Cracow, raising tomatoes. She told me where there was a hole in the fence. When the Germans came for another selection, they took to the gas chamber my sister who was eight months pregnant, and my other sisters, but I ran away to Cracow and went through this hole to freedom. The boss registered me to work, so I was a free man.

"But I still had a hole where my right eye should be. Then I read in the paper that a German doctor was coming who could put in an artificial eye. So I took a risk. Kaminsky is a Polish name, so I took off my Star of David and went to the hospital. I came in with my boots on like the Poles, and I spoke Polish to him, so he thought I was Polish and he made me an artificial eye.

"I worked at the airport about a year, and then came two big trucks and they loaded eighty of us onto the trucks. The driver said, 'We're going to Our Father,' so we thought they were going to shoot us. But instead we came

87

to a factory and saw this tall, beautiful man—Oskar Schindler. The factory was making pots and pans and later mess kits for the army. I fed the pigs and raised geese, and if Schindler found out a horse broke a leg, he bought the horse for us to eat, too. Once he had a party for German bigshots, and one got drunk and wanted to shoot some Jews. Schindler came to us in the kitchen and said, 'Run away, leave everything, run!" He walked on two sides—working for the Germans and helping the Jews.

"In 1945 we heard the Russians were coming closer, and Schindler wanted to move us to Czechoslovakia. He went to Himmler with a list of 400 women and 700 men, and said he had to have the same Jews because they had experience for this kind of work. The other Jews in Cracow were sent to Grossrosen, but we went to Brinitz, where I worked in the kitchen until liberation.

"When the Russians came, Schindler told us to take the materials from the factory because the Russians were going to take it anyway. I filled up a big truck and went back to Cracow, and sold the material. I saw a girl carrying two little pans, walking to ask the Jewish Committee for a little bit to eat. I knew her because my parents used to have orchards, and her family would come in summer to the orchard. We got married on January 27, 1946.

"We wanted to immigrate to the United States, but we couldn't go from Poland, so we smuggled ourselves into Germany through Czechoslovakia. It was February, and we went through water and snow in the forest. Eventually we got to Munich. I had a little store selling cigarettes, American coffee, this and that, and the Jewish Committee got me an apartment. In 1951 we came to New York."

HINDA DANZIGER KIBORT

KOVNO, LITHUANIA

"Frau Schmidt taught us to have real perspective. When we were humiliated, or hurting or cringing inside, when they called us 'animals,' she said we should remember who was the animal and who the human being: 'The real animal is the one that humiliates another human being.'"

Hinda Danziger's father was a designer in a shoe factory. She was nineteen when the Germans marched in and announced, "The Jews are not human beings." She witnessed S.S. guards murdering her mother.

"Because my parents came from Riga, Latvia, they spoke Russian and German fluently," said Hinda. "We children spoke Lithuanian, Yiddish, and German. I attended a very good private school where most of the teachers had come from Germany. Starting in January 1933, when I was twelve, Jewish students were not allowed to participate in sports activities and were always pushed aside. By April I had to leave the German school and enroll in a Jewish school.

"In June 1940 the Russians marched into Lithuania and the government was overthrown. Property owners and people who were in business became 'undesirable elements.' When the Germans marched into Lithuania in July 1941, school had let out for the summer, so our whole family was together, including my brother who was at the university and my little sister who was in tenth grade. We tried to leave the city, but it was just like you see in the documentaries—people with their little suitcases walking along highways and jumping into ditches as German planes strafed, coming down very low and killing people. We were on the road but German tanks overtook us, and we had to return home.

"We did not have time like the German Jews did, from 1933 until the war broke out in 1939, for step-by-step adjustments. For us, one day we were 'human,' the next day we were 'subhuman.' We had to wear yellow stars. Everybody could command us to do whatever they wanted. They would make us hop around in the middle of the street, or they would make us lie down and step on us, or spit on us, or they tore at beards of devout Jews. There was always an audience around to laugh.

"One night they came in the middle of the night and arrested all the Jewish men, including my father. Unless one had an awful lot of money for bribes, there was only one way to get somebody out of jail, and that was if he was absolutely needed to run a business or a factory.

"The very large shoe factory where my father worked had been taken

Hinda Kibort (with bow in hair) with her parents, brother and sister, and an uncle

over by the German military, and they had put a Lithuanian in as director. I went to that Lithuanian and asked him if my father could be released. He grabbed me by the neck and threw me out.

"I came home and announced that I would go directly to the Germans to try to get my father released. My mother and her friends thought I was crazy! But I went to the headquarters building and waited and waited. While the guard was changing, I just opened the door and went in.

"Inside stood a stocky man with gray hair, and I heard people addressing him as 'Herr Commandant.' So I said, 'Herr Commandant, may I have a few minutes?' I spoke German like a native, with no accent, and he gave me five minutes! I explained aout my father and he asked me how I had learned to speak such perfect German. 'In school, Herr Commandant,' I said. 'Because you speak such beautiful German I will help you,' he said. And he wrote me a paper in red pen that said, 'Danziger is to be released.'

"I ran home, and I shouted, 'Papa is coming home!' You should have seen my mother and those other women whose husbands had been arrested! They put me on a chair, and one brought me water, and one stroked my cheek. They thought I had gone out of my mind. But my father came home the next day!

"In September all the Jews of Shavl were enclosed in a ghetto. We lived together in little huts, sometimes two families to a room. There were no schools, no newspapers, no concerts, no theater. Officially, we didn't have any radios or books, but people brought in many books and they circulated. We also had a couple of radios and we could hear the BBC, so we were very much aware of what was going on with the war. As long as we were strong and useful, we thought we would survive. Everybody had to go to work except children under twelve and the elderly. There were workshops in the ghetto where they made earmuffs for the army, for instance, but mostly people went out to work in nearby factories. We were guarded all the time. A few people tried to escape, but were caught. We did not know yet about concentration camps.

"In 1943 the war turned, and we could feel a terrible tension from the guards and from Germans we worked with on the outside. We could sometimes exchange clothing or jewelry for food, but this was extremely dangerous because every time a column came back from work, we were all searched. Once they found some bread and a few cigarettes in the pocket of a baker coming back from work. He was hanged on a Sunday. There was a little orchard in the ghetto, a public place, and we Jews had to build a gallows there and a Jew had to hang him. We were all driven out by the guards and made to stand and watch this man being hanged.

"November 5, 1943, was the day all the children were taken away from our ghetto. The Germans brought in Romanian and Ukrainian S.S. to do it. All five of us in our family were employed in a factory adjacent to the ghetto, and we could see through the window what was happening. When we came back after work we were a totally childless society! You can imagine parents coming home to—nothing. Everybody was absolutely shattered.

"People were looking for answers, for omens. They turned to séances or to heaven to look for signs. And this was the day we first heard the word Auschwitz. There was a rumor that the children had been taken there, but we had never heard the name so we thought they were saying 'Der Schweiz,' the German word for Switzerland. We hoped that the trains were going to Switzerland, that the children would be hostages there but would be OK. We were wrong.

"On July 16, 1944, the rest of the people in the ghetto were put on cattle trains, with only what we could carry. We had no bathrooms. There was a pail on one side that very soon was full. It was very crowded. The stench and the lack of water and the fear, the whole experience, is just beyond description.

"At one point, when we were in open country, a guard opened the door and we sat on the side of the car and let our feet down and got some fresh air. We even tried to sing. But then they closed the door, and we were all inside again.

"When we arrived at Stutthof our family was separated—the men to one side of the camp, the women to the other. My mother and sister and I had to undress. There were S.S. guards around, men and women. In the middle of the room was a table and an S.S. man in a white coat. We came into the room in groups, totally naked. I cannot describe how you feel in a situation like this. We were searched, thoroughly, for jewelry, gold, even family pictures. That's when I lost my very last possession, tiny photos of my family. I was holding them between my fingers, even when I was naked, but when they made us stand spread-eagle, the photos fell to the floor and were lost. The guards looked through our hair, they looked into our mouths, they looked in our ears, and then we had to lie down and they looked into every orifice of our bodies, right in front of everybody. We were in total shock.

"From this room we were rushed through a 'shower room.' There were little openings in the ceiling and water was trickling through. In the next room were piles of clothing, rags, on the floor. You had to grab a skirt, a blouse, a dress, and exchange among yourselves to find what fit. It was the same thing with shoes. Some women got big men's shoes. I ended up with brown suede pumps with high heels and I used a rock to break off the heels so I could march and stand in line on rollcalls.

"After this we went into registration and they took down our profession, scholastic background, everything. We got black numbers on a white piece of cloth that had to be sewn on our sleeve. My mother and sister and I had numbers in the 54,000s. People from all over Europe—Hungarian women and Germans, Czechoslovakians, Belgians. There were no children. When families came with children, the children were immediately taken away.

"As prisoners of Stutthof we were taken to outside work camps. A thousand of us women were made to dig anti-tank ditches, a very deep V-shaped ditch that extended for miles and miles. The Germans had the idea that Russian tanks would fall into those ditches and not be able to come up again! When we were done digging, 400 of us were taken by train deeper into Germany. We slept in tents, fifty women to a tent. We had no water for washing and not even a latrine. If at night you needed to go to the bathroom, you had to call a guard who would escort you to this little field, stand there watching while you were crouching down, and then escort you back.

"We were covered with lice, and we became very sick and weak. But Frau Schmidt, a woman in our group, helped us to survive. She was a chemist, and she taught us what roots and grasses we could eat that weren't poisonous. She also said that to survive we had to keep our minds occupied and not think about the hunger and cold. She actually made us study every day! We took turns giving talks.

"Even now I remember Russian poetry she taught to us when it was her turn to lecture. My friend and I spoke about lectures we remembered from school. The talks that were hardest on us were from Lorna who came from Belgium. She always spoke about food. We called the day when it was her turn to speak, the day Lorna 'cooked.'

"By the middle of December we had to stop working because the snow was very deep and everything was frozen. On January 20, 1945, they made a selection. The strong women who could still work would be marched out, and the sick, those who couldn't walk or who had bent backs, or who were just skeletons and too weak to work, would be left behind. My mother was selected for this second group and my sister and I were given the option to stay behind with her which we did.

"We were left without food, with two armed guards. We thought the guards might burn the tents, with us in them! Then we heard there was a factory where they boiled people's bodies to manufacture soap. But the next day the guards put us in formation and marched us down the highway until we came to a small town.

"We were put into the jail there. There we were, ninety-six women standing in a small jail cell, with no bathroom, pressed so close together we couldn't sit down, couldn't even bend down. Pretty soon everybody was hysterical, screaming. Then slowly we quieted down.

"In the morning when they opened the doors, we really spilled outside! They had recruited a bunch of Polish guards and they surrounded us totally, as if we were in a box. Ninety-six weak, emaciated women, marching down the highway with all these guards with rifles. Suddenly the German guards told us to run into the woods. The snow was so deep, up to our knees, and most of us were barefoot, frozen, our feet were blistered. We couldn't really run, but we spread out in a long line, with my mother and sister and I at the very end. I was near one guard, and all of a sudden I heard the sound of his rifle going 'click.' I still remember the feeling in the back of my spine, very strange and very scary. Then the guards began to shoot into the group.

"There was a terrible panic, screams. People went really crazy. My sister and I always held hands with my mother in the middle, but now she let go of us and ran toward the guards, screaming 'Don't shoot my children!' They shot her, and my sister and I grabbed each other by the hand and ran into the woods.

"We could hear screaming and shooting, and then it got very quiet. We were afraid to move. The guards wore those terrifying-looking black uniforms with the skull-and-crossbones insignia, and every tree looked like another guard! A few women came out from behind trees, and eventually, ten of us of the ninety-six made it out to the highway.

"With our last strength, we walked to a small Polish village about a mile away. We knocked on doors, but they didn't let us in, and they started to throw things at us. We went to the church, and the priest said he couldn't help us because the Germans were in charge. We were so weak we just sat there on the church steps, and late in the evening the priest came with a man who told us to go hide in an empty barn. We did not get any other help whatsoever from that whole Polish village—not medical help, not a rag to cover ourselves, not even water. Nothing.

"The next morning a terrible battle raged right in front of the barn. We were so afraid. Then it got very quiet. We opened the door, and we saw Russian tanks rolling into the village. We were free!

"The Russians put us into an empty farmhouse. They gave us Vaseline and some rags, all they had, to cover our wounds. Then they put us on trucks and took us to a town where we found a freight train and just jumped on it. At the border Russian police took us off the train. They grilled us, 'How did you survive? You must have cooperated with the Germans.' It was terrible. But finally we got identity cards. My sister and I decided to go to the town where we had lived. We thought somebody might have survived.

"In Vilna station a Jewish doctor said we were the first survivors he had seen. He told us, "Don't go back to Shavl. They'll kill you! There are no Jews left in small towns in Lithuania.' When we said we were going on, he ran to some Russian officers and two of them took us off the train, so my sister and I stayed in Vilna. In October 1945 we heard that our brother and father had survived.

"To get out of the Soviet Union was impossible at that time. But the Zionist underground managed to get us documents saying that we were Polish citizens, and in 1946 we were allowed to 'return' to Poland. Then we crossed the mountains on foot into Czechoslovakia and took a train to Germany.

"I worked in Munich for the Central Committee of Liberated Jews, which administered all the Jewish displaced person camps in the area. There I met my husband-to-be, who is from my hometown. He had survived Dachau and came to Minneapolis in 1947, I came in 1951, and we were married.

"I was a prisoner from age nineteen to twenty-three. I lost my mother and twenty-eight aunts, uncles and cousins. To be a survivor has meant to me to be a witness. Silence would not be fair to those who did not survive.

"There are people who say the Holocaust never happened. We must keep talking about it, so future generations won't grow up not knowing how a human being can turn into a beast, not knowing the danger in keeping quiet when you see something wrong brewing. The onlooker, the bystander, is as much at fault as the perpetrator because he lets evil happen.

"When someone asks me, 'What can I do?' I say, 'When you see something bad happen to people who can't stand up for themselves, get up and say, 'This is wrong.' Write to the newspaper or your congressman saying, 'This should not happen in my community,' and sign your name. Then maybe somebody else will have the courage to come forward and say that he protests, too.'"

REVA KIBORT

WARSAW, POLAND

"A lot of people say, 'Why didn't you fight back?' Well, when a soldier comes over to you with a gun, with a German shepherd dog you're not going to fight back because you know he will kill you in an instant."

Very few children who were imprisoned in concentration camps by the Nazis during World War II lived to tell their stories. Reva Kibort is one of the few who did.

When the Nazi army entered Poland on September 1, 1939 Reva Mandelbaum was just six years old. She and her five siblings survived weeks of bombing in the Germans' attempt to level the city but, says Reva, "my father was killed right away."

"At first the German's weren't too bad. Once they came into the city, I remember standing in line for food. They were handing out soup and bread and I remember standing in line with my sisters and mother and they gave me a piece of bread and some soup and they were pretty decent. . . . we thought, oh well, maybe it won't be so bad.

"Needless to say, it got worse and worse. Finally, in 1940, the ghetto was started. They built the ghetto with a wall around it. They asked the Jews to move into a certain area and you had to move out of your own home and move into somebody else's. They assigned you apartments where, if you would normally have one family, they had two or three or four families.

"Naturally it was very, very, crowded. There was no sanitation. They started giving out rations for food. We couldn't get any food. And slowly, they systematically tried to choke us all in the ghetto. Then came disease—typhus—people got sick and started dying. I remember as a little girl, walking out of the gate I saw dead bodies—children and mothers—it was awful. The starvation was unbelievable. And I remember one day especially. I was very, very hungry and I came in and told my mother that I was so hungry, and she said, 'Go out and play. If you play you'll forget you're hungry.' I remember I had this great big rubber ball and I went out and played a little bit but the hunger didn't go away. I don't think that you've ever felt hunger unless you've been on a starvation diet—the hunger is so painful.

Soon the deportations began, said Reva. "They started taking the young people and eventually all that was left in the ghetto were old people and children. A lot of people say, 'Why didn't you fight back?' Well, when a soldier comes over to you with a gun, with a German shepherd dog, you're not going to fight back because you know he will kill you in an instant."

Reva and Ben Kibort

Slowly the Nazis evacuated the Warsaw Ghetto. "Every week they would come to homes and take the people out," said Reva. "And eventually, on July 8, 1942, that was the last evacuation of all the Jews. On that day, they took away my mother and my sisters and my aunt—everybody."

Before the final liquidation, Reva's mother had urged her daughters Eda and Reva to flee and try to join their sisters Ann and Mindel and brother Mark who had already escaped from Warsaw. "We really didn't want to go," said Reva. "But my mother said to us, 'Why don't you go ahead and I will follow you?' Needless to say, she didn't follow. By the time she was ready to follow, the Germans came and took her away."

Reva and Eda escaped through a hole in the ghetto wall. "It's so funny but you know what? The Germans didn't even look at us! We were two little girls, I was eight years old and Eda was twelve. We smuggled through the wall to the Aryan side. And when we finally got to the Aryan side, my sister Ann was there and my brother, and my other sister. We were hoping that the gentiles would keep us because we had brought them a lot of things that we had taken from the ghetto. Well, during the night, a guy got drunk and he started calling us 'dirty Jews'… and he came with a hatchet and he was going to kill us all, but he was too drunk. So my oldest sister Ann took me and the others and we ran out of the house in the middle of the night and ran into a field and hid in the corn."

In the morning the siblings boarded a train for the 50-kilometer ride to their parents' home town. "I sat on that train for maybe a couple of hours as a mute," said Reva. "I didn't speak Polish because I'd never gone to school. My only language was Yiddish. We all sat on the train pretending that we were non-Jews."

When they arrived at their destination, they found that the village Jews had all been rounded up in the town square. Reva and her siblings, who were mistaken for Christians, were not allowed to enter. But one of their uncles spotted them and the children joined the group as they waited for deportation to the slave labor camp at Deblin. In 1944, with the Russian army approaching, they were transferred to another camp in Czestochowa, closer to the German border.

It was at this camp that Reva experienced one of the most horrific experiences of her life. Upon arrival, said Reva, "they divided the men, women and children. There were only eleven children left from the other camp. I was the oldest of the eleven and I was eleven years old."

"The Germans had all the women disrobe because every camp had a different uniform. So I watched what all the women were doing, getting disrobed, putting on different uniforms and then going into the barracks. I was holding a baby who was born in the previous camp, a six-month-old little girl, and a German yelled at me, 'Throw the child away and run.' Here I was, a blonde little girl, sort of a cute little girl, thinking that I looked like a gentile little girl and for that split second, I think the German had a heart. I don't know what it was, whether I reminded him of his grandchild, maybe of his own child. I don't know but he told me to run and I put the baby down. I ran into the pile of dirty clothing and a German took his machine gun and in front of me killed all the ten kids —boom, boom, boom. I ran into the barracks and all the mothers came running over to me saying, 'What happened? Where are the kids?' And I don't know... I didn't tell them that the children were killed. I wouldn't tell them. I just didn't have the heart."

In Czestochowa Reva was assigned to the ammunition factory, washing bullets. She worked there until the Russians liberated her on January 17, 1945 at the age of twelve.

GISELA KONOPKA

BERLIN, GERMANY

"In the Resistance there was no glory, no reward. Even distributing leaflets was death. I stood in my solitary cell and said, 'The worst thing is that nobody will ever know that I was a decent person.'"

When the Nazis came to power in 1932, Gisela Peiper was a college student. Almost immediately, she joined the anti-Nazi Underground. She and her husband escaped to France, and then in 1941 to the United States. She became internationally known for her research and writing on adolescent psychology.

"During the First World War, when my father was in the army, a woman came running into our store and said that the baby who was the Christ child in the Christmas tableau was sick and could she borrow our little Ruth, my baby sister," said Konopka. "My mother said, 'Certainly!' It was beautiful, my sister lying in the crib with all the angels around her, and they all loved my mother and loved us.

"But when the war ended in 1918, anti-Semitism really started. Swastikas were painted on the streets, and we would scratch them off with our pocket knives. I was eight years old when one of the girls in my class drew a swastika on the blackboard. The kids said, 'Gisela, you have to go and protest.' But there was one Jewish teacher, and she was very afraid and told me not to make trouble. I started to cry and went home, and my father said to me,

'Gisela, you'd better learn that Jews are here for suffering.'

"By 1932 I was studying to be a teacher. The Nazis began marching through the streets, carrying spades. They were not allowed to carry weapons, but if you said something against them, the spades would fall on your back. I am definitely a product of the Weimar Republic, a time of great excitement and social conscience. We distributed leaflets against the Nazis, but even some Jews said, 'Oh, it won't be so bad' or 'At least we'll get rid of the labor unions.' My God, we read !

"By 1933 Jewish professors had been dismissed, and the day before my final exams, the Nazis searched my room and threw out every book. During the exam, a Nazi in uniform sat at the table. I vomited, but I passed my examinations with superior grades. Paul Konopka and I were very much in love, but he was not Jewish, so we were not permitted to get married. Then a person asked whether we would be willing to work with the Underground.

"People in America do not understand the word 'totalitarian,' the horror of living in a society saturated with fear. There was incredible terror, no communication with anybody you hadn't known before, so it was very important that people knew there was a Resistance movement. Nothing was in the newspapers, only how wonderful the Fuhrer is, so we distributed leaflets, pasted slogans on walls. We were in groups, at most five people you knew and could trust, Jews and non-Jews together. The first people the Nazis arrested were Socialists and Communists. They were beaten, humiliated, made to scrub the streets with toothbrushes.

"Then in Hamburg in 1936 there was that ring of the doorbell in the night for me. I was at that time one of the major contacts to others. I swallowed their names on paper very fast, without water, and in marched three young storm troopers. I pretended to be very surprised. They tore apart everything in my room, especially the books. Then they said, 'You come with us!' They stopped at another place for a young woman of the same Underground group, so I knew somebody had given us away.

"The first night they put us into what I would call a standing coffin, a box. It was dark. I couldn't sit, I could only stand. I heard men screaming, 'Let me out, let me out! I'll tell you what you want.' But I have a very good imagination, and I was in a meadow, the sun was flooding it. And later, when a young S.S. was standing in front of me with a flood of dirty words, I thought, 'I'm wearing a raincoat, and it's just running off me.'

"The Hamburg prison was filled with political prisoners. I was there six weeks which seemed like an eternity. I lived through it by saying hundreds of poems to myself, reading whole pages of books without having the books. One old jailer gave us hot soup, and there was one woman who did things to make life a little easier for us. But Christmas night I heard them pulling out one person after another and beating them mercilessly. And once, in front of me walked a woman whose hands hung in a totally distorted way. I could see that her hands were broken. One day I heard a lot of shouting and looked out a peephole and saw with my own eyes a man being literally hunted to death, like an animal. They made him run, then jump, run, lie down, jump, throw himself down, jump up, until blood spurted out of his mouth and he was dead.

"Then one day they called me in and said, 'You can go home,' and shook my hand and said, '*Auf wiedersehen.*' They had told me at the last interrogation, 'You will never get out of here,' so I knew what they wanted. They wanted me to lead them to others who would then be caught.

"I went back to Berlin. My father had died. I got my mother out of the country, to my sister in Palestine. And in my life have been miracles. I walk in a street and see a young Jewish woman I know, who looks beautifully suntanned. I say, 'Where have you been?' She says, 'Karlsbad, in Czechoslovakia.' I knew that, like me, she had no passport, and I said, 'How did you get out?' She told me there was a doctor at the Czech embassy who would write out a certificate that you are sick, and they let you go! He looked at me with big, sad eyes, and he wrote how desperately ill I was. Not a cent he asked, and I never knew his name.

"I lived in Czechoslovakia about a week, mostly on hot water. Then the decision was made that I should fight the Nazis in Austria. Another woman was doing the same thing, so we move in together. Then she was caught, and we both were put into a horrible prison in Vienna, dirty, filthy. But it was police, not Nazis, and finally they let me go. One day an old woman, crying, handed me a leaflet saying that the Germans were coming. That night the Vienna sky was filled with smoke, everybody burning material that was dangerous, and German planes were circling, circling, circling. I went to say good-bye to the Jewish people where I had been working taking care of their children. The furniture had already been demolished by Austrian Nazis.

"I had seen bad things in Germany, but in Austria the Nazis were drunk with victory. They knew they had the world! I was in a strange state of shock. I walked through the city and I thought, 'If I ever come out of this, I want to tell what it was like.'

"I got a false passport and got on a train to France. Paul was in Paris, poverty-stricken and eaten by vermin, but alive. I worked as a maid, then a governess, then a refugee committee gave me a job. Then the idiot French arrested all the German refugees, their best friends, including Paul. And then it was bedlam, bombs falling, and the Germans were coming.

"I squeezed in a train moving south, to Montauban. Montauban was like a miracle. Catholics, Protestants, the entire city opened their homes, gave us false papers, rations, all the things we needed. I was very sure I had lost Paul for all eternity, and then he met somebody who knew where I was, and we were reunited. Paul became a woodcutter and we lived in a stable. We ate blackberries and suet and bread, and farmers gave us milk.

"The life of a refugee is especially horrible if you were used to being important, part of the Underground. We wanted to stay there and fight, but everybody said, 'There have to be witnesses,' and so, between the Unitarian Service Committee in Marseille and the Jewish Socialist Labor Committee in New York, we came to New York in 1941.

"The committee arranged for us to go to Pittsburgh, so I could go to school to study social work. Paul was an ironworker and a welder, and then he went into the American army for three years, back to Europe, while I studied and gave a lot of speeches about the Nazis. In 1947 I came to the University of Minnesota to teach.

"People try to understand how what happened in Germany could happen in a country that had produced Schiller and Goethe and Beethoven. There was terrible inflation and enormously high unemployment, and they wanted someone to blame, like the intellectuals, the Socialists and Communists, and the Jews. There were Germans who were good people, who fought the Nazis and died, but if the lie is big enough, and you make good propaganda, most people accept it. And then you give the power to the murderers.

"The child says, 'I am going to school,' and the mother says, 'You can't go to school, they'll spit at you.' The child says, 'I'll spit back,' and the mother says, 'You can't because you are a Jew.' This is the way one teaches children to be afraid. What we can learn is never to raise children to blind obedience and never to hate a group or a race."

MANFRED KLEIN

POSEN, GERMANY

"Before 1939 Hitler was quite willing to let the Jews leave Germany. The hard part was to enter other countries. America wouldn't take Jews; other countries didn't want Jews either."

Posen and the territory around it became part of Poland after World War I, and residents could choose whether to be Poles or Germans. The Klein family moved to Breslau, in German territory. In 1938, the Nazis arrested Fred and his father. They were Germans, but they were also Jews.

"There was always slight anti-Semitism in Germany," said Klein, "but German Jews were assimilated. We thought of ourselves as German citizens of the Jewish faith. In 1933, when the Hitler movement came, people were afraid, but Germany was a democratic country so we weren't very worried. We thought 'If he is voted in, we will be able to vote him out.' We were wrong.

"We were very careful after 1933 who we talked to. Among non-Jews parents didn't even trust their own children not to deal with Jews, and vice versa. The Germans allowed a certain percent of Jewish children in certain schools, and I had to fight my way both to and from school. I was fifteen.

"I was a member of Zionist youth groups, a citywide leader. We had to divulge the membership of our groups and let the Gestapo know where our meetings were held. Jews weren't permitted to go to university, so when I graduated I went into the family business.

"In July 1938 there was a big roundup of so-called 'criminals'—Jews who were married to gentiles or had a gentile girlfriend or boyfriend. Then in November, on Kristallnacht, they destroyed everything Jews had. Our business was destroyed, everything smashed. Our bank accounts were closed and all valuables had to be handed over to the Nazis. There was a three-day roundup, and my dad and I were arrested. We were shipped to Buchenwald by passenger train under heavy guard. Nobody resisted. If they did, they were dead.

"At the main gate to Buchenwald we had to run a gauntlet, about 100 yards between two rows of S.S. men having fun cursing us, hitting us with sticks, and trying to trip us. We didn't listen, we didn't look back, we were preoccupied in running and getting out of their way so we didn't get hit. I also had to protect my dad, who was sixty. I kept him in front of me to see that he didn't fall. Anyone who fell and was too weak or too old to get up was beaten.

"We were 10,000 men crowded into five huts, like army barracks. Inside were tiers of bunks five high, just enough room to crawl in. We had nothing to do all day. We got watery soup and blood sausage to eat. Orthodox Jews weren't supposed to eat the sausage because they weren't kosher, but the rabbis told them they should because preserving life comes first.

"When people went to the infirmary they didn't come back, so our own Jewish doctors treated us. One man had an appendix operation during the night by a Jewish surgeon who was also a prisoner. He operated by candlelight, using a pen knife.

"When you see the tower with machine guns pointed at you, you know you can be killed. For the slightest offenses we were punished, and sometimes for no reason at all. They punished us with what they called the Sachsengrusse, standing on our tiptoes for two or three hours with our hands behind our head. Other prisoners had to lie over a saddle mount and got fifty or seventy-five lashes with a whip. One prisoner escaped and they captured him, so the next day we had to watch his execution on the gallows. Of 10,000 people, 2,000 died in the nine weeks we were in that camp.

"Ransom for our release could be paid to the German government by confiscation of our property and by money raised in other countries, so in December they started letting us go. My father was in the first batch they released, people over sixty, and people who had been German soldiers in World War I and had been awarded the Iron Cross.

"Then they released those who had proof that they could leave the country. My mother got me a permit to go to Sweden to be trained in farming, so I could go to Palestine. Five friends and I were released together on January 13. We left the camp by truck, and went to Berlin by train. The first thing we did in Berlin was get drunk!

"Unfortunately, I didn't really have a permit to go to Sweden; it was a fake! So I had to stay in Berlin. All of us young people went to the Jewish community center in Berlin, trying to find ways of immigrating to other countries. I met my future wife there and we became engaged. Meanwhile, I had friends who went over the 'green borders' through the forests into Czechoslovakia or Holland or France. But if they were caught by border guards or the police, they were handed over to the Gestapo.

"Finally I got a permit to go to England as an agriculture student, and my fiance got a nursing permit. On July 17, 1939, we went to England. We were married in London in October, one month after war was declared.

"I could communicate with my mother and father through Sweden by 24-word Red Cross notes. For a while I got notes and letters back. Then in 1943 my parents were taken to Auschwitz, to the gas chambers.

"In the concentration camp I became an atheist. I was angry at God. I wouldn't even enter the synagogue. But my wife wanted the synagogue in our lives, and slowly I softened up, when my son was born, and later on for my grandchildren."

BEREK LATARUS

LODZ, POLAND

"They told my sisters to go away, to give the little child to my mother. My two sisters didn't want to leave her. One took her arm from one side, and the other from the other side, and the four of them walked to the crematorium together."

Berek Latarus worked with his father in the family lumber business after graduating high school, buying firewood by the carload and selling it to bakeries and factories. He could have stayed behind as a laborer when the Germans liquidated the ghetto, but he chose to go with his family to Auschwitz. He is the only survivor of his family.

"When we heard the Germans were coming, everybody ran out into the street," said Lataurus. "We saw them on their motorcycles, with the dogs and everything, and it was kind of fun watching an army come in. Our parents said, 'Ah, we know the Germans. It will be the same as it was in our war (WWI).'

"Average people were really not afraid. They didn't know what was going on in the world. They were occupied with work, with children. But right away the Germans burned the synagogue. Lodz had one of the most beautiful synagogues in the world, and they burned it to the ground. Then they took some Jewish people—women and men—and hanged them in the market by their feet with their heads down, to show us we should be scared.

"They made a ghetto, strangled us around with barbed wire. We couldn't go out but we were afraid to escape anyway. Where could we go? Everybody was working for the Germans in straw factories and shoe factories and clothing factories. I was doing deliveries for the Germans, straw, food, fabrics to the clothing factories, in trucks and by horse-and-buggy. We got stamps for groceries, maybe two or three pounds of potatoes a week for a whole family, one loaf of bread, some horsemeat. We couldn't live on it, and we couldn't starve on it!

"We used to see people who didn't work swollen from not eating, dying on the sidewalks. In the ghetto we knew everybody. We had friends who died. There were mass funerals. There was a curfew, and rules that we couldn't assemble. On every Jewish holiday, the Germans sent people to concentration camps. The first to be taken were educated people—doctors, lawyers. Then they took the older people who were not able to work. In 1940 the Germans threw the children out of the windows onto trucks. I saw them do it. In Poland people used to save gold and diamonds. That was their security. But the Germans knew which Jewish family had gold or diamonds. The one in charge used to be in the same business as my father, so he knew what we had. I had to take everything my father had hidden and give it to him. Otherwise they would have killed me.

"The day they liquidated the ghetto they told us to take whatever we could carry with us. But when we came to the boxcars, they didn't let us take anything, just chased us into the boxcars and closed the doors. We rode for two or three days with no food, no water. At one station, they opened the door for fresh air and some of the Polish people tried to give us water. None of us knew where we were being sent. We thought they were shipping people to Germany or somewhere else in Poland to work. Nobody knew about Auschwitz or concentration camps, or the ovens.

"In Auschwitz, the first thing they did was separate women from men. Then we had to take off our clothes to take a shower, and when we walked out of the shower they gave us a pair of wooden shoes and the uniforms with the stripes—pants and a short jacket. In the barracks we slept on a burlap sack with straw inside, on a bunk, until four or five o'clock in the morning. Then they woke us up so they could count us and select us for work. Our barracks was close to the crematorium, and we could smell that smoke from the chimneys.

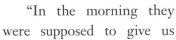
Berek Latarus

"In the morning they were supposed to give us coffee, but if the kapo didn't like you, he would just pour it on the floor and tell you to wipe it up. They gave us a piece of bread that was supposed to last two or three days. If you ate it up, the other two days you starved, but if you didn't eat it, someone might steal it from you. I saw with my own eyes, sons stealing food from their own fathers. People don't realize what hunger means.

"In one camp I was working in the kitchen so I had enough to eat, but in other camps I was like anybody else. One time I stole a bread and they took me to shoot me, but a non-Jewish guy from Cracow, who was my friend, ran and took me away from the Germans! This non-Jew was on good terms with the S.S., he used to smuggle them cigarettes, and we called him the 'Jewish father' because he stuck up for us all the time.

"To survive you had to be lucky, keep yourself clean, stay healthy. We had just the one uniform, never washed, never cleaned, but you could wash with cold water sometimes. Some people were so depressed they didn't take care of themselves. People who got sick, you never saw them again. I never got sick.

"To survive you also had to always look like you were working, like you were digging or something. Some people couldn't work, and then we heard the guns. And you had to use your head. People who were smokers used to sell their soup for a cigarette. These people didn't survive. And some people were so religious they used to go into a corner during the day to pray. If the S.S. caught them praying, they were through, too.

"From Auschwitz we were sent to Regensburg, locked in boxcars for days. There were people in the boxcars so hungry they couldn't control themselves. They would bite the flesh out of dead people. Near Regensburg we worked on the railroad to clean up every morning from the Allied bombing. One day we saw planes coming. Our guards ran away, and the bombs fell right where they hid. They were killed and we were free! I ran with two friends, and we hid in a cemetery. An old woman gave us food and clothes and told us to go away, but German civilians surrounded us, and took us back to camp.

"Later people from our camp walked for weeks to another part of Germany. I was still with people from my town, relatives, friends, people I grew up with. My three uncles were very strong guys, but they got sick and couldn't walk anymore. The Germans shot all three. Everybody was waiting for their turn. I really didn't think about surviving; I thought that I was going to die. We were walking through this little town, Laufen, in May 1945 when some farmers came running out on the highway, saying, 'The war is over!'

"There was an army camp not far from there, and it became a displaced persons camp. Then later four of us guys moved into a house, We opened a Jewish center and I was president. HIAS and UNRRA helped us. People started leaving to look for relatives. I knew my immediate family had gone to the crematorium, but I looked for aunts and uncles. I couldn't find anybody. The sister of one of the guys I lived with came looking for him, and I married her in 1947. In 1948 our daughter was born. My brother-in-law and I opened a fabric store. My wife had a sister who had come to the United States, so that's why we came.

"I was really bitter about the Germans after the war, but you change. There are good people, there are bad people. Hate doesn't do any good. I believe in God now. When my children were growing up, there were nights I couldn't sleep. I dreamed I was still in Auschwitz and could still see everything. It was heartbreaking, and I used to cry. I really couldn't talk to my children about it, but my children and my grandchildren, said to me, 'Tell me.'"

MARK MANDEL

WARSAW, POLAND

"We looked like the Poles, and we spoke Polish, my sisters and I. People couldn't identify us as being Jews. This was why we survived."

Moshe Mandelbaum was only nine years old when the Germans came to Poland. To survive, he and his sisters begged, stole, smuggled, and traded gasoline, coal, cigarettes, and other items. After the war he went to Palestine and in 1948 he fought in Israel's War for Independence.

"My father was a shoemaker with nine people to feed," said Mark. "I had six sisters—I was the only boy. One sister worked as a seamstress, another as a store clerk. They helped out, but we knew hunger. My father was a self-taught person, very much involved in politics, and I remember people gathering around him discussing events of the time, like the civil war in Spain.

"It was unusual for Jews in Warsaw to live in a gentile neighborhood, but my father took this particular apartment because it was a storefront in a big apartment complex, a whole block. The gentile boys always used to attack us. In September 1939 was the first air raid in Warsaw. We lived near railroad tracks and my father was afraid they were going to be bombed next, so we moved in with my aunt. For about a week it was quiet, so my fifteen-year-old sister and I went back to our apartment to clean it up, so the family could move back. In the afternoon there was an air raid again. My father saw smoke billowing from the direction where we lived and ran to save us. He was killed in the air raid.

"We took care of my mother. We were all capable children, resourceful, aggressive. To this day I can't believe the things I did at the age of nine, ten, eleven. At the railroad station, gasoline was spilling out of some tankers, and we took home gallons of it and sold it. We kept it in the single room where we lived—a big open tub filled with gasoline! We would go to the railroad yards,

Mark Mandel

and my sister would jump on a moving coal car and throw out coal for my other sisters and me to pick up, so we got coal to heat and to sell. We once saw a guy carrying a big sack of peanuts in shells, and my sister grabbed it and dragged it home. We bought cigarettes wholesale, and we'd sell them. When the Germans marched into Warsaw they were passing out bread and you were supposed to get only one, but my sister somehow got three.

"We looked like Aryans and pretended we were gentiles, but people knew we were Jews. Early in 1940 there was a directive from the Germans that all Jews living in our area must vacate their apartments. We found an apartment in a Jewish area, our first Jewish neighborhood. This was the start of the ghetto.

"We had a nice large apartment, but we were rationed, deprived more and more of material things and food. A lot of people burned their furniture to keep warm. We were smuggling, going through the wire barriers to the gentile side, buying things and bringing them back into the ghetto.

"There was no transportation in the ghetto except a streetcar that went through two blocks of it on its way through the city. I used to get onto the streetcar on the Christian side with my merchandise, and as the streetcar was going the two blocks through the ghetto, I'd jump off. And many times my sister rode the streetcar with a suitcase of merchandise—flour, sugar, different things—and I would jump on the streetcar, she'd hand me the suitcase, and I'd jump off!

"One night I was out smuggling and got stuck on the Christian side after curfew. I was wearing knickers and I had them full of caramel candies, to be sold in the ghetto. I was only eleven, but I spent that whole night alone in a burned, bombed-out building. Another time I got caught by a Polish policeman. They threw me in a jail with a bunch of drunks, but the next morning they let me go because I spoke Polish like they did, and they thought I was a gentile.

"I once saw a German guarding the gate to the ghetto, and a Jew walked by, innocent, not bothering anybody, and the guard just shot him, just like that. Then a cart went by, and they threw the body on just like merchandise, discarded. I saw the Germans load a group of old people, sick people, on the streetcar, take them to the cemetery, line them up and shoot them down with machine guns. I saw it with my own eyes, looking out our attic window.

"During this time, the Germans were systematically taking Jews out to the Treblinka death camp. They promised people a pound of jam and a bread if they'd come to the station to be 'relocated.' We never fell for it, but my mother's sister did, with her little girl, five years old. She was never seen again.

"The ghetto was getting smaller and smaller. My sisters Eda and Mindel and I did the dealing and the smuggling, and we decided to go to the town where my parents had come from, Deblin. My youngest sister, five years old, had died of a kidney infection. I took my sister Ann over to the gentile side and put her up with friends—Polish Christians who knew we were Jewish. The following day we went to get my mother and my other two sisters, Masha and Reva, and take the train to Deblin. But my mother told us to go ahead, with Reva. 'I'll come, I'll follow you,' she said, but my mother and Masha never came.

"So now we were left alone, four sisters and me. We were with our gentile friends in Warsaw, but it was getting uncomfortable because some people knew we were Jewish and were blackmailing us. Then the Germans decided to eliminate most of the Jews who were left. I got caught with a group of Jews being marched, like cattle, to the train for Treblinka. My sister Eda was walking on the sidewalk as a Christian, saying, 'Let him go, he's not Jewish.' And I was telling the Germans, 'I'm gentile, I'm gentile! I'm not Jewish! Let me go, please!' Finally they let me go, and I ran with my sister.

"We bought railroad tickets and went to Deblin, not knowing that Deblin was already completely 'Judenfrei'—free of Jews—except for a labor camp next to the railroad station. My uncle and one of my cousins were in that camp, so we smuggled ourselves in! But in the camp they were weeding out the Jews, too, taking them away. I sat in the toilet the whole night, and my sisters were lying in a dumpster outside the camp. After midnight I came out and my uncle wasn't there, he'd been taken away. My cousin was gone too.

"My sisters climbed out of that dumpster and came into the camp, and we became laborers. I was assigned to a bunker to preserve potatoes. The Germans dug huge holes with bulldozers and put the potatoes in. Then we put on straw and then dirt, and then more potatoes and straw and dirt. My sisters worked in the greenhouse.

"I was still a tough little kid. I stole a big aluminum pipe from a plane that crashed near camp and gave the pipe to a sheet metal man, so he could make cooking pots. I got one for free, and the rest he sold. I went around picking up cigarette butts and saved the tobacco to sell to people who smoked. I learned German, and during my breaks I cleaned the Germans' houses, fixed things, polished their shoes. So we got money and we bought bread.

"Really, we were not hungry. There was a huge public kitchen, and everybody could go and cook. We smuggled potatoes, and my little sister Reva cooked supper for us when we came home from work. We thought we were the only Jews left in the world.

"Then the Russians started advancing, and the Germans decided to load the 600 people in our camp on railroad cattle cars, but with open doors, not cooped up. The guards sat in there with us. We went to Czestochowa, and as we were unloaded, they took what little we had away from us.

"We lived there for six months, producing bullets for the German army, but the Russians kept advancing, and on January 16 the Germans marched us into a huge warehouse to load us onto trains. Then I saw airplanes flying and bombing, and the Germans ran to hide. Hours went by and the railroad cars were still waiting for us to be loaded, but the Germans didn't come. The next day we were liberated by the Russians. We went into the house of the German leader and burned it. We raided the warehouse and found bread and two cans of honey. One of my sisters and her boyfriend and I started hitchhiking away from the front. We saw dead Germans, burning, tanks running over them. My sister was almost killed by a drunken Russian thinking she was a very attractive girl. We hitched a ride in a truck, and the truck fell into a huge anti-tank ditch the Germans dug to stop the Russian tanks. Through all these experiences, it was as though somebody was watching over us.

"We slept on Polish farms, being very careful not to tell the Polish people we were Jews. Then we came to a railroad station where we had a feeling that other people there might be Jewish, too. The password was 'Amcho,' from the Hebrew words for 'our nation.' We'd ask 'Amcho?' and if a person said 'yes,' we knew he was Jewish. We found out my mother's cousin was alive in Lublin, so we took the train there and went to my cousin's house.

"My other three sisters who were still alive came to Lublin, too. Three of us went to a Jewish orphanage where we were fed, got new clothes, started school. Then I found out some children from that orphanage were meeting secretly with a Zionist organization trying to recruit children to go to Palestine. I joined and went with the group to Feldafing, and we were taught Zionist ideas, and Hebrew writing and reading. My two older sisters married, but for my two younger sisters and I, our goal was to go to Palestine.

"In April 1946 the British government allowed a thousand surviving children from concentration camps to go to Palestine. I was selected! I came to my sister and told her, 'Guess what! You're going to find me with a shovel on my shoulder, building Palestine!'

"I was assigned to a kibbutz named Kfar Nahum. Half a day we went to school, half a day we worked. I chose construction because I wanted the feeling of building the country with my toil and my sweat. I also joined the Haganah at the age of seventeen. We were training with rifles, and early one morning as the sun rose I gave the oath and became a member of the Haganah. It was a very proud moment, knowing that I was putting my life on the line for Palestine.

"In 1948 I fought in the War for Independence. Before we went to battle they'd ask us who to notify if we got killed, and I was really sad because my sisters had gone to the United States and I didn't have anybody in Israel. On February 3, 1955, I was granted a visa to come to America.

"Many times I feel guilty that for 2,000 years the Jewish people dreamed of returning to their land, and I'm sitting here in America. I try to make it up by giving money to Israel, but it's not enough. I really should be in Israel.

"In our minds my sisters and I were always hoping we would see our mother, or our sisters, or our cousin or uncle. Until this day, although I know it's never going to happen, I always hope I'll see a face I'll recognize as one of my relatives!"

ALLEN MASTBAUM

DUBIENKA, POLAND

"You sit inside that bunker. If somebody finds you, you're going to die. Every second, every minute, for two years, you think about death, you talk about death. Nobody can imagine what this is like."

When the Germans occupied Poland in 1939, Allen Mastbaum was sent to Belzec as slave labor. Later, en route to Sobibor, he and hundreds of fellow prisoners broke through the sides of the wooden cattle cars and tried to escape. Most were shot, but Mastbaum survived and hid in a bunker for two years, until the war ended.

"In 1938 we heard that in Germany they had started to attack Jewish people," said Allen, "but all the old people remembered 1914, the First World War. 'When the Germans came,' my father said, 'the Germans didn't touch anybody, just put us to work, but they didn't kill.' That's why we didn't run away. But then it was a king, Franz Josef. This time it was Hitler.

"In 1939 the Germans crossed the border and the Russians came in, across the River Bug, and then the Russians moved back and the Germans occupied us. Right away they took about ten people, the best people from downtown, and started a Judenrat. The Germans told the Judenrat what to do. For instance, if they wanted a million dollars, they would say to the Judenrat, 'You have one week to get us a million dollars, otherwise 10,000 Jews will be shot.' And the Judenrat had to collect the money.

"In the ghetto were apartment buildings with maybe a hundred Jewish families. I saw with my own eyes when the Germans came with a big truck and parked by the windows, and they threw the children through the windows into the truck! The mothers couldn't bare it; they jumped, too.

"In 1940 they took about 300 young people from our town to Belzec, a place where they repaired trains. There was also a mill to grind wheat for flour, and a factory to which we would bring wood to be cut into boards. There were 20,000 people in Belzec. They gave us a little piece of bread and black coffee in the morning, and at noon a little bit of soup with a bone from a horse. The Judenrat brought us packages of food every week.

"When the guards took us to work we saw the Russians across the border. A German would take your cap and throw it to the Russians. You'd run to pick it up, and he'd say, 'You're running to the Russians, across the border,' and he'd shoot you. They shot twenty, thirty people that way.

"We were in Belzec for a year. Then war broke out with the Russians, and they put us on a train to Sobibor, a death camp. We were in a cattle car, day and night, people dying on the floor. About five kilometers before Sobibor, the train stopped. We knocked out a wall in the cattle car, and we started jumping out. On the train roof were Gestapo with machine guns, and they start shooting. There were maybe a thousand people lying dead when the train started moving.

"I felt myself all over, and I wasn't hit! I said to myself, 'I'm alive!' and I crawled out from under the dead bodies. When you want to live, it makes you very strong, and I ran to Chelm, where there was still a ghetto. The Judenrat gave me a work card.

"I was there until 1942, working in a kitchen peeling potatoes. One day I heard that they were going to take all the Jews to be shot. I took off at midnight and found some people to take me in a horse and wagon to my brother, about twenty kilometers from Chelm. I said to my brother, 'The Gestapo is going to kill everybody, so let's go to the woods.' My brother had a gentile friend who had fought with him in the Polish army. The friend had a big farm near the woods, and my brother paid him to help us dig a bunker. We worked all night and all day, dug the hole, cut trees, and put leaves and grass on top. On November 28, 1942, we went into the bunker. We were there almost two years, my brother, my sister, her little girl—four years old—and me. We got water from a creek. My brother had gold pieces, so every week his friend brought loaves of bread and we'd pay him.

"Then one day my brother went to where he had some things hidden, and someone brought the Gestapo and they shot him. I'd gone with my brother, but I'd stayed outside, and I could see everything. I ran back to the bunker and told my sister what happened.

"In summer 1944 the Russians came. I was afraid a tank would fall into the bunker and kill us, so I stayed outside and watched from behind a bush. I could see flames from the city, and the Germans running away. We came out of the bunker, barefoot, in rags. In town the Polish children ran after us, laughing, making fun, hollering, 'Jews still alive! Jews still alive!' A couple of Jews got shot, so we saw this was not a place to stay.

"We went to Waldenburg, in the Russian zone. In Waldenburg everything was expensive and in Chelm everything was cheap, so I would buy butter in Chelm and sell it in Waldenburg. I was on the train when a Polish organization took about thirty Jews off the train and killed them. One Pole shot a Jewish woman, and her little girl started crying, 'Mother! Mother!' and he shot the little girl, too.

"I said to my wife, 'No more Poland!' We went to Ulm, a displaced persons camp. I knew I had two uncles in America, my father's brothers. I knew their names but not their address. I addressed the envelope just 'Jewish Organization, New York,' and after four weeks I received a letter and a package of clothes from my uncles in St. Paul, Minnesota! So we came to America."

HELEN MASTBAUM

SKALAT, POLAND

"Just bad dreams are left me, nothing else. I hear my husband screaming and yelling, and I wake him up and say 'What happened?' And he says, 'They pulled me by my hair, they want to kill me!' It's been so many years, and the Germans are still part of us."

From age twenty, Hinda Kornweitz worked for the German occupiers as a tailor's assistant. When the last Jews in Skalat were killed and the ghetto burned in 1943, she hid in the woods with other refugees until she was liberated by the Russians in 1944.

"My father had a little store selling pails and dishes, like a hardware store," said Helen. "We were religious people. We didn't understand much about anti-Semitism, but when we used to go into the park, Polish kids would throw stones at us.

"We were close to the Russian border. In 1939 we were very happy that Russians occupied us because we heard rumors that Germans would kill Jewish people. But then the Nazis came. The first day they took 600 men who never came back.

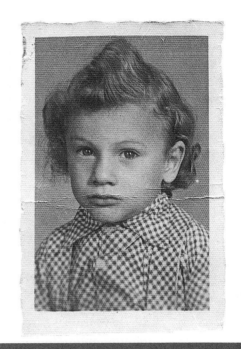

Helen Mastbaum

"My brothers were both in the Soviet Army, and my father hid in the cellar. A German officer came and opened my closet and saw men's suits. He wouldn't believe they were my brothers'. He started beating me and I started screaming, but then another soldier stopped them. They took me and my sister to work in the field. My father came out of his bunker, and they took him to work in the kitchen because he spoke a little German.

"In 1942 they made a ghetto in our city. A gentile family took our house, and we went to live in their house, sixteen people in a very small house. I lived with my younger sister and my father's sister and her children until they were all killed. We sold clothes, furniture, everything we could to survive. We sold a bedroom set for ten pounds of potatoes, a little flour and a chicken.

"One morning the ghetto was surrounded by S.S., shouting, 'Raus, raus!' I was always lucky, hiding when they made this kind of search, and they never could find me. That time we hid in the attic, and after three or four days we heard people talking, voices we knew, talking about families that had been taken away.

"Then it was back to work in the fields again until a neighbor, who worked as a tailor for the Germans said to them, 'I have a daughter who can help me in my shop.' And they believed I was his daughter and gave me a card so I could work with him.

"About three or four months later, I heard shooting and I looked out the window and I saw everything on fire in the ghetto. I ran out the back door and hid in a stable in the hay. Finally I had to go out to find food. I went to my father in the labor camp in Skalat. I crawled under the wire and came to my father's cabin. I hid there with him and my father brought me food. Then one day he told me the Nazis were going to search, and he took me to a gentile woman who had a bunker in her kitchen. She hid me for two weeks.

"One day she told me the Nazis had killed my father, and that they were going to kill everybody in the camp, so the city would be completely Judenfrei. When it got dark, she gave me water and a piece of bread, and I started walking. Then I heard somebody behind me. It was a Jewish man and a woman, so we were three. For a week we hid in the fields by day and walked during the night, until we came to the woods. There we heard voices of people we knew! We made a bunker. It's hard to admit this, but we stole. We dug up potatoes, picked corn and beets. At night we made a fire to bake potatoes. There was a group of five, one of three, and one of seven living in the woods. We helped each other.

"We were in the woods nine months, until March 1944. Then, for twelve days we were surrounded by fighting. We could hear Russian, we could hear German. We were afraid a tank would come and crush us in our bunker, so we took turns watching. Then one day we heard Russians speaking, and we came out. It was March 14.

"We started walking to the city. Everything was bombed, and Russian and German soldiers lay dead in the streets. The gentile woman who was living in my house was surprised to see me! I told her I'd like to see my house, stay overnight. She made me sleep on the floor, treated me very badly. Polish people were very mean to us and I was afraid. I was sick in the hospital for two or three months and when I got well, I went to the police, and they made that woman give me back my house.

"Finally, I went to Gliwice, where I met my husband in 1945. We went to Poland to a displaced persons camp, and we started writing letters to family in America. My husband's uncle sent us papers to come to the United States."

ROSE MEYERHOFF

BRUSSELS, BELGIUM

"Each time the S.S. searched the convent grounds, the nuns would alert us and we children would leave our classrooms and start running in the opposite direction. We had to keep quiet and go fast, and we were very afraid."

Rose Jacobowitz was only seven when the German army occupied Belgium in 1940. When the Germans took her mother away, a neighbor took her to a Catholic convent, where she was given a false name and attended school until the war ended. At age fifteen she came to the United States, alone, to live with an aunt and uncle she'd never met.

"I knew the war had started because draft registration for the army was in our school," said Rose. "My mother and I packed up and ran, to avoid the oncoming German army. Jews, Catholics, hundreds and hundreds of people were leaving Brussels, and we didn't stop until we got to Paris. My parents were divorced, and my father, a cabinetmaker, was living in Antwerp. I had a sister living with my aunt and uncle in Antwerp, and they were supposed to meet us in Paris. Then we were going to get on a boat to England. But we never made contact in Paris, and we couldn't get to the North Sea because the borders were closed, so we went back to Brussels. Later we found out my aunt and my sister were hit by a bomb and killed. I don't know what happened to my father.

"In September I came home one day from school, and a friend of my mother's stopped me at the door and said, 'The Germans were here. They took your mother away. Don't go upstairs to the apartment.' I trusted him, so I went with him to the train station and we traveled to Louvain, where Benedictine nuns were running an orphanage for Catholic children. There were Jewish children already there when I arrived, and more kept coming. We were each given a Christian name. Mine was Christiane DeGraef.

"Every morning we would file into the chapel, looking all alike in our black dresses, and say Catholic mass before breakfast. At first the Jewish children could sit in back and not participate, but later the nuns got nervous, and we were asked to kneel, and stand, and sit, and open the prayer book, like the Catholic children.

"The Catholic priest who ran our program was shot by a firing squad because he allowed Jews to attend, but the nuns decided to keep Jewish children anyway. Periodically, the Gestapo would come to the convent and say they had heard there were Jews hiding there, and they insisted on searching the convent grounds each time.

"The convent was quite a large building, laid out in four squares with a courtyard in the middle, and about four stories high. Each time the Germans came, we would leave the classrooms immediately with one of the nuns. If Nazis were coming up one staircase, we would go down another. So we were always out of sight of them, and they would be satisfied, and leave. They came probably six or seven times to search the convent grounds. It just sounds fantastic, I know, that a hundred kids could go up and down the stairs and not be discovered. But when I went back to visit in 1974, there were a couple of nuns still there who had taken care of us, so then my husband believed me!

"We knew when the liberation was coming because one teacher had an underground radio. She came every day with a map and little colored pins, so we could see the English and American armies advancing through France and Belgium. We laid the map on the floor and crouched behind her desk, hoping nobody would look in the windows and see what we were doing. In the afternoon we would stand in the courtyard and count the Allied bombers, sometimes 200 at a time, flying over on their way to Germany. Louvain started getting bombed, and if the bombs came at night, we would run down to the basement and lie on the floor and try to sleep.

"One night we looked out the window and saw white dots coming down from the sky, like snow. Pretty soon we could see that these were parachutes. We ran outside and there were jeeps and tanks and trucks filled with soldiers. We were hugging each other and screaming and jumping because we knew that we no longer had to worry about getting killed, or caught, or sent away.

"In January 1945 I left the convent because Jewish organizations were trying to find Jewish orphans. Nobody really knew what to do with us, though, because we were too young to be sent off into the world on our own. I was sent to a Jewish orphanage in Weisenbaek. In April of 1947 HIAS located my mother's brother, who had come to New York in 1922. They told him his niece had survived in Belgium, and he and his wife adopted me.

"I was in the convent for two-and-a-half years, and I still have a special feeling for Catholics, and nuns in particular. They risked their lives for us."

VICTOR MINTZ

WARSAW, POLAND

"The brain is a computer. You start a new life but you can never erase, never forget. You lost dear ones, friends, you raise children with no aunts and uncles, no cousins, no grandparents. But life is life. It goes on."

Victor Mintz was descended from men who were both scholars and successful businessmen. He escaped the Nazis by fleeing to Russia, then Lithuania, then back to Russia.

"My father passed away when I was two years old, and I was raised by my grandfather from my mother's side, Moshe Sander Engelman. His was one of the best-known Jewish families in Poland. About half of Poland's woods belonged to his father; his business was cutting and exporting lumber. He was a religious Jew.

"When the 1914 war started my grandfather took us to the Ukraine, to Pruszkow, because it was dangerous in Warsaw. Then, one Sabbath afternoon in 1919 Ukrainian Cossacks killed 5,000 Jews in three hours in a pogrom. I saw them through the window, running with swords. After, we had a hospital in our house with over 100 injured people. I was ten years old.

"In 1922 we came back to Warsaw and I graduated high school, and then went to business college. I became the main accountant in a bank.

"Life was very harsh for Jews. Even at the University was a fight because they wanted Jewish students on the left side of the room and Poles on the right. I remember a big Jewish student demonstration.

"In 1937 Jewish businessmen started to boycott German products. In 1938 the Germans deported all the Jews who used to be Polish citizens, and a lot of those refugees came to Warsaw. There were a lot of Talmudic schools, Hebrew schools, secular schools in Yiddish, Zionists, Socialists, Bundists—it was like a rainbow.

"On September 1, 1939, the war began. They called us on Sunday morning, September 3, to dig trenches in the heart of the city. We came—and there were no shovels. Nobody knew what to do, so we went home. On Monday morning, September 4, my two cousins and I walked out of the city, going east. Along the highway airplanes were coming down very low, with machine guns shooting, and to the left and right of us, people died. We would run into the woods when we saw planes coming. For five or six days we were walking and running on the highway. I went to Bialystok and stayed till the end of December, Then I smuggled across the border to Lithuania because Lithuania was still a free country. I was caught crossing the border. It was Saturday morning, and it was still dark. The Lithuanian soldiers took me and the other two boys to the border to send us back to Russia. We saw a Jew on his way to synagogue, and I told him the soldiers wanted money, so he told the soldiers to come to the synagogue, and they paid the soldiers so the soldiers let us go. In the middle of the night, the Jews took us by horse and buggy to Vilna, then to Telz. There I got a job as accountant in a factory, and I got married.

"In June 1941, the Russian-German war started, and we started to run again, going by foot. Again on the highway, German planes came down with machine guns shooting. And Lithuanian partisans were also killing Jews. We took a freight train to Kovno, then to Riga. The Germans were already in Riga, but by a miracle, the train depot was on the Russian side.

"There was chaos. Nobody asked who you were, or where you were going. We took the train to 200 miles before Moscow. The train stopped every fifteen or twenty minutes, and people got off, because German planes were bombarding the train. But we came safely to a collective farm near Danilov.

"I was there a couple of months working, and then I saw that the front was coming nearer. Also it started to get cold, and we didn't have any warm clothing, so my wife and I decided to go south to Samarkand. We didn't have food, we were sleeping on the streets. But finally, I got a job. My daughter was born in Samarkand.

"In May 1946 the United States and Russia agreed that all Polish citizens had to be let out of Russia. We came to Lodz, all the Jews were gone. In Warsaw I didn't find Jews either.

"I had heard about the Holocaust, but now I could see it! I looked for relatives, friends, I couldn't find anybody. I heard that my sister and brother-in-law and their little baby were killed; they died on the way to the camps. My mother had died. My grandmother, I don't know. By the gate at the cemetery was a little stone, the grave of my grandfather. He had passed away a few months before the liquidation of the ghetto. Who put up the stone? I don't know.

"Most of the houses were gone, but my apartment was not destroyed. A man was living there, and I asked if I could see my old rooms. 'Yes,' he said. 'You've got a lot of books in the basement.' But I was afraid to go down in the basement with him because I thought he might kill me. I had heard about the pogrom in Kielce, where Poles killed many Jews after the war.

"Our idea was to go to Palestine. But it was illegal and I had a little daughter. My wife two brothers and two sisters who went to the United States before the war, so in 1948 we came to America."

HENRY OERTELT

BERLIN, GERMANY

"Brown-shirted S.A. troops were marching down the street, singing, 'Once the blood of Jews squirts off our knives, everything will go twice as well.' It was a very frightening thing for a small Jewish child to listen to."

After Henry Oertelt's father died, his mother worked as a seamstress to support her two sons. Henry went to trade school at age fourteen to study furniture design and was apprenticed to a furniture maker.

Henry Oertelt (right)

"I grew up in a neighborhood that was predominantly gentile," said Oertelt. "I was the only Jew on the soccer team at school, and soon after Hitler came to power, I was made to know that I'm not welcome on the team anymore. When Hitler came it was not a sudden thing, it had been growing since 1921, but everybody was frightened. People with money had a chance to escape, but we were poor, and my mother's work diminished more and more as Christian people were not allowed to have contact with Jews. Beginning in 1941 we were forced to wear the big yellow star with the word Jew written across The law prescribed that these had to be sewn on in tight stitches, and an S.S. man, or one of the brown-shirted S.A., or just a plain policeman would stop you, take a pencil out of his pocket, and try to get the pencil under and between the stitches. If they could, you were taken right to the Gestapo and sometimes were never seen again.

"Being a teenager, I made a star out of tin, glued material over it, soldered a pin in back, and stuck it into my jacket, I wore this thing away from the house, and then I just took it off, hoping that nobody would stop me. I also did not obey the curfew law much. I'm not trying to show that this was brave. It was actually pretty stupid.

"Jews were not allowed to have radios or record players, bicycles, cars, pets. I remember when we had to turn in our pets, the old ladies walking in the street carrying their birdcages, tears running down their cheeks. In summer Jews were not allowed to be on the street after nine, in winter curfew was at eight. No Jew was allowed to go to the movies, theaters, restaurants, any public places. We could use public conveyances only to go to and from work.

"As a teenager, the thing that hurt me most was giving up my record player and records. But a Christian friend sneaked to our house carrying his record player with records and a bag of food. We would play the music with blankets over our heads, so the neighbors wouldn't hear us. And when it came time for us to be sent to the concentration camp, he even offered to hide us.

"Berlin was not a small place. It had four-and-a-half million people, so to get around was not easy. But young people want fun, so the group that I belonged to—musicians and so on—would get together at one of our apartments on Saturday afternoon, make music, do all kinds of things, and stay overnight.

"Jews were put on ration cards before anybody else. When the rest of the population was put on rations, Jews' food rations were cut lower. We had to buy clothes on rations, and it nearly took all year's ration points to buy a pair of socks. For Jewish workers, half the wages went into Hitler's treasury, and out of the other half taxes had to be paid, so there wasn't much left to live on.

"In 1939 almost all Jews were removed from their professions—lawyers, doctors, businessmen, and in my case furniture maker. We were put on street work, shoveling dirt, rolling and carrying rocks. All we had were hand shovels and four-wheeled wagons we had to pull with ropes or leather straps.

"Most Berlin Jews lived in apartments, without even a yard to dig in, so they were very, very unhandy with tools. We were also a very odd-looking group. Next to me worked a tiny man, not young, a very famous surgeon in Berlin. He came to work in the only clothes he had, a double-breasted, blue-striped suit. He couldn't even go out and buy himself a pair of work pants because of the rations. He was carrying rocks, with those tiny hands. It would have been a most comical sight, if it wasn't so sad.

"Kids on school field trips would come by, and the teacher would stop and point and talk, and the kids giggled. Where they would normally see a crew of tough hard-hats, they saw a bunch of comical-looking people like this little doctor, dragging wagons. Hitler wanted to prove to the German population that Jews were subhuman, and these kids were being taught to kill something that was of no value.

"For two years I did street work. Then in 1941 Hitler found himself short on skilled help, so he took people like me and put us back into practice. I was put into a factory, with my own workshop, to make furniture for some big-wig Nazi.

"Pick-up 'actions' for concentration camps were increasing, so when you went to bed at night, you almost anticipated that you would not be there in the morning. Sometimes they would come to factories, load the Jews onto trucks, and haul them away.

"Apparently this big-shot I worked for had enough power to say, 'Hey, I need this Jew who makes furniture for me, so leave him alone.' But in March 1943 the inevitable happened. About two in the morning we heard gun butts banging on the door, and there stood two S.S. men in their black uniforms, with a dog. You expected it but you still didn't believe it, so when it really happens you run around crazy, throwing things into suitcases. We had fifteen minutes, no more.

"We were taken to a waiting truck and hauled to a collection center, a burned-out synagogue. When there were enough people for a transport, we were brought to the train station and I was on my way, with my brother and my mother, to our first concentration camp.

"In those days, Theresienstadt was one of the milder camps, controlled by Czech police who tried to keep their distance. Women were separated from men, but I could see my mother sometimes in the evening.

"There were no gas chambers yet in Theresienstadt. They didn't need them; people died of starvation and sickness. Lice, fleas, bedbugs all had a feast, and there was no way to get rid of them. People could not resist scratching, and would die of infections.

"The smell from the bakery in Theresienstadt lingered over the whole town, but it was a tease. When our food was dished out, we got a piece of white bread three by three inches. Usually we got soup, dished out of huge barrels. You learned that the guys who dish out the soup didn't bother to stir it, so if you weren't one of the first in line, you had a chance of getting a nice hunk of sludge, instead of just water, in your bowl. People would dig in garbage bins to find a piece of rotten bread or vegetable.

"After about a year in this place, my brother and I were ordered to the train station. Guards with gun butts, fists, and sticks shoved us into cattle wagons like sardines. This is how I came to Birkenau, to Auschwitz.

126

"We were tattooed. It was then announced that there will be no more names used. If you were asked what your name was, you were to answer with your number. Particularly in the beginning, as you stood nervously for head counts, a guard would come toward you and tap you on the shoulder and say, 'What is your name?' And in your nervousness, you would blurt out your name. By the time you got yourself off the ground with his boot in your belly, you'd remember you're supposed to say your number. So you look at your arm because you forgot your number, and that's when you get another kick, because you're supposed to remember.

"Another favorite game of theirs was to go to one of the prisoners, grab his cap, throw it out of the guard lines, and order the prisoner to retrieve it. Every prisoner knew that if he stepped out of the guard line, he'd be shot. But we also knew that if we didn't obey orders they'd beat us to a pulp. So what to do? You have the eternal hope that there may be a glimmer of humanity in somebody's heart, and you step out of line to retrieve the cap. And you always were shot.

"From Auschwitz we were taken to Flossenburg. My brother and I talked to each other a lot to keep ourselves sane. Also, we recognized that our only chance for survival was to work because they weeded out the sick people and took them to the gas chambers. That's what happened to our mother. I got an infection, a swelling under the arm, big as a tennis ball. My brother was taken out to work, but I was hopelessly sick. I saw that I had no chance of survival with this infection.

"At the sick barracks were long lines of guys with swellings on their bellies, their faces. They were weak, starved skeletons. I saw a doctor tell a prisoner to put his foot on a stool, and when the guy faltered, the doctor smashed his fist in the guy's face. Then he took his knife and just slit the growth open, and pus spurted out, and that was it.

"Finally my turn came. Prisoners were crying and shaking and asking for help, and I figured that the German militaristic posture is always to be stiff and straight and short-speaking. I was in terrible pain and weak, too, but I spoke in very short, militaristic words and stood straight, and the doctor's eyes opened wide, and he said, 'We will give you anesthesia.' Well, it was a big operation, and I have a big scar. I stayed in the sick barracks, from which they sent the very sick people to the gas chambers, but that doctor would always pass me. I was the only one he was nice to.

"From Flossenburg we were sent on a death march, and after about two-and-a-half days I was liberated by a contingent of Patton's Third Armored Division. I weighed eighty-two pounds. The Americans in those armored vehicles opened the hatches and threw us food, the ration boxes American soldiers got. It was a wonderful thing, but also regrettable. We scrambled for them like crazy —cans of meat, fat, butter with oil swimming on top. Some of the guys sat right down and tore the boxes open and stuffed themselves with both hands. Many got dysentery, and it couldn't be stopped. They died from that food.

"Fortunately, my brain was still working. I opened some Saltine crackers and ate a few of those, and I only took a little tiny piece of the chocolate. Then American medical teams came and took over, and the food boxes were taken away.

"We were assigned to farmers' houses, and the farmers were ordered to take care of us. Then the war was over, and I decided to walk to Berlin because we had planned that, if we survived, we would try to get home. It was a 700-mile trek, and I was picked up by some military vehicles, but a good stretch of it I walked.

"At the end of June I arrived in Berlin, but my brother didn't come. The walls of the Jewish organizations were covered with slips of paper, 'I'm looking for so-and-so.' 'Does anybody know the fate of. ..' I put up notes, too, but heard nothing. I married a girl I knew from before the war, a young girl who used to say 'hi' to us teenagers. And then one day a fellow comes by and says, 'My gosh, you're lucky. Your brother is alive in Munich!' Knowing the physical shape I was in when we separated, my brother never even looked for me!

"Our apartment was in the French sector of Berlin, and the French did not allow anybody to leave except to go to France. France wasn't far enough away from Germany for me; I wanted to go to America where my brother had gone. Finally, by buying false papers, we moved into the English sector and came to the United States in 1950.

"Most of the Germans were terrible, but some helped. After the war, if I was asked to be a witness. against the doctor who operated on me in Flossenburg, I would have had to tell the truth. He killed other people, but he probably saved my life."

SAM RAFOWITZ

WARSAW, POLAND

"By-fifteen-and-a-half they took me already. I went to work one day and I never came home."

Sam Rafowitz was born in Warsaw, the capital city of Poland. With one-third of its 1.2 million residents Jewish, Warsaw had the largest Jewish population in Poland. Like teenagers everywhere, fifteen-year-old Sam enjoyed a life of school, sports and spending summer holidays with his bubbe (grandmother) in her town about 60 miles south of Warsaw.

In September 1939, when the Nazis entered Poland, Sam witnessed the beginnings of the brutality to come. He saw old Jewish men attacked in the streets and their beards cut off. By November 1939, Nazi authorities required Jewish citizens to wear white armbands with blue Jewish stars. Jewish schools were closed and Jewish property was confiscated.

By October 1940, the Germans had established the Warsaw Ghetto. All the Jewish residents of Warsaw were forced to move into this area of the city. Ten-foot-high brick walls were built, topped with barbed wire, and the ghetto was sealed off and guarded.

The Nazis forced Sam to clean out ghetto apartments. "By-fifteen-and-a-half they took me already. I went to work one day and I never came home," remembered Sam. "They loaded us on trucks and we didn't know where we were going. We found out the place was a concentration camp, Majdanek, in Lublin." When the truck full of men first arrived in Majdanek, the Germans were not yet ready for them. So Sam and the others spent their first night in the cold sleeping in an open field.

In the morning they were issued uniforms, and their heads were shaved, the beginning of Sam's 20-month imprisonment at Majdanek. Over the next five years Sam was forced to work as slave labor in five concentration camps—Majdanek, Auschwitz, Buna, Dora and Bergen-Belsen. He built roads and assembled rockets and munitions for the German military. "Every day in Majdanek was another day of survival. . . . Every day they examined you naked. If you had a little meat on, you were still useful and were sent to the right. If not you went left, you went to the crematorium."

While Sam was imprisoned at Majdanek, his mother and his sister, Helen, were imprisoned in the Warsaw Ghetto. Almost 400,000 people were forced to live in the 1.3-square mile ghetto. Overcrowding caused disease and starvation. By August 1941 nearly 5,000 people were dying every month. One day, while working at Majdanek, Sam saw a group of women and he thought that perhaps his sister Helen might be among them. He convinced a German guard to let him look for his sister. He found her and they made a pact that should they survive the war, they would meet at their home in Warsaw.

Sam saw his mother for the last time in Majdanek. He glimpsed her in a group of women. She recognized him —and tried to give him her sweater. She was immediately shoved back into line by a guard. It was the last time Sam ever saw her.

In 1943 Sam was transferred to Auschwitz, where he was imprisoned for two years. In Auschwitz he received his tattoo —number 129552. "This was my name. When you got your number, you went to work. They brought in Gypsies, whole families with wagons and horses. For seven days the chimneys of Auschwitz smoked constantly. At night we used to see the chimney going and we used to say, 'Where is God, where is God?'"

"Many times at night we thought about how we might run away. Where will we run? It was not easy. A Polish family would not take you in, you had on a striped suit. You could go into the woods if you could make it through the wire, but if you touch it, you're dead."

By January 1945, one of the coldest winters in Polish history, the Germans learned that the Russian army was approaching. As the Allies advanced, the Germans took the prisoners on a seventy-kilometer death march. At night, while the majority of the prisoners slept out of doors, Sam and his group were allowed to sleep in a shack. This meager shelter kept him from freezing to death during the night. "There were lots of deaths in the night. It was twenty below zero." Their final destination was Bergen-Belsen.

The British army liberated Bergen-Belsen on April 15, 1945. "I heard the announcement that we were free! A whole army liberated the camp.

Thousands and thousands of people were there. I couldn't even walk anymore because for two weeks we hadn't had any food. The soldiers saw me and they rushed me right away to the city to a Catholic hospital. I could not digest food. They kept me there for six weeks. I weighed 78 pounds when I was liberated."

May 8, 1945 was Victory in Europe (VE) Day. The war was over in Europe and the survivors began their search for family members. As Helen had promised her bother, she returned to Warsaw to find him, but he wasn't there. Sam was still hospitalized in Germany. By November Sam was strong

Sam Rafowitz

enough to search for Helen. He learned that she was with a group of survivors in a displaced persons camp in Judenberg, Austria. He began a journey that that took him across the continent from Bergen-Belsen through Austria and finally to Regglio Emilia, Italy.

When Sam arrived at the camp in Regglio Emilia, "there was a guard. He looked at me and said, 'Are you Helen's brother?' Just like that! I said, 'Yes. Is my sister here?' He said 'Yes.' We went into a small room where people were learning Hebrew. He said, 'There is your sister.' I saw a beautiful young girl. We hugged and she was shocked because they had told her I was killed trying to escape. That is how I found my sister."

Sam and Helen returned to Bergen-Belsen, the former concentration camp that now served as a large displaced persons camp. It was there that he met his wife, Cyla Bonk. They married there and their first son, Ivan, was born. Sam and his family immigrated to the United States in 1950.

LIBBY ROSENZWEIG

BRESLAU, GERMANY

"After the war I went back to my hometown. Our Christian next-door neighbors had taken our home, everything we had. They wouldn't let me in even to take a look".

Libby Storozum was thirteen when the war began. As a slave laborer in German factories, she says she did not know real hunger or mistreatment. But she still has nightmares about the horrors she witnessed.

"My father came from Poland," said Libby. "He spoke German and Russian and Yiddish. He had a fruit store in Breslau, but when the Germans came to power, he moved us to Modrzejow. He went back and forth to Breslau until 1935, when the Germans took our passports away. Then we had a stand selling live fish in the market on Thursdays and Fridays.

"The first we knew the Germans were coming was when we saw the gorgeous synagogue across the river on fire. Then we knew it wasn't just war against Poland; it was war against the Jews. We went to stay with my father's family, five kilometers away. Then S.S. troops with black uniforms and red armbands began gathering all the Jews with beards. My father had a beautiful beard, and my sister went for a barber to cut his beard, while I went to get bread. That was where my horror started because the streets were paved with bodies, with open skulls and bellies.

"I wore a white armband with a blue Star of David, and then I had to wear the yellow Star of David on front and back. We were enslaved. We dug ditches, cleaned the Germans' quarters, their villas. We heard that they were moving the Jews closer together into ghettos, so we packed a suitcase and a knapsack.

"They came early in the morning. I spoke German, so the caretaker took me to be the interpreter for our three buildings, even though I was only fifteen. I heard one S.S. say to the other, 'If half the family is in the work camp, the other half can go free.' I didn't tell this to my parents, I just volunteered to work, and my parents were sent home. I didn't know that later they would come again and my parents would then be taken.

"They gathered 5,000 of us in a field, and I was one of sixty girls selected to go to a spinning factory in Arnau, Czechoslovakia. We went by regular passenger train. On the train I had my sixteenth birthday. In the labor camp we were all aged thirteen to eighteen. We didn't have any freedom—there was barbed wire—but we were not treated badly. We had a female German work commander, a Jewish camp leader, and a Jewish nurse. The flax came in big spools, and I had to bring it through water and gears onto little spools. We were making cloth for soldiers' uniforms.

"We worked every day except Sunday, when we had to clean the factory. In the morning they gave us two sandwiches, one for breakfast and one for later on. Much of the food was made from thickened blood and horsemeat, and being from a Hasidic home, I didn't eat those things.

"I was in labor camp for almost two years. In March 1944 our director told us the small camps were being closed, so he was going to transfer us to Bernsdorf, a paper factory. Bernsdorf was run by S.S. We all got numbers, the yellow star with a number and a red triangle. That's all we were, numbers. The S.S. were brutal. If they caught somebody doing something they didn't like, they beat us. If the American military succeeded, they beat us. They brought in girls from Auschwitz with striped clothes and shaved heads, who told us about the horrors of Auschwitz. We lived in fear.

"Seeing the girls from Auschwitz, I didn't care anymore. I let the machine go. They threatened to send me to Auschwitz, to kill me. But instead they put me in a sewing room. I wasn't a seamstress and I didn't know how to do it right, but I had a beautiful voice and I was singing, and the girls helped me so I would be able to make production quotas and the S.S. wouldn't send me away.

"I was lucky with food, too. I was assigned to a machine with the manager's wife, and she felt so sorry for me that in the morning she would put a sandwich with butter on top of the machine for me. I could understand Russian, and when we were liberated by the Russians I protected her.

"Just a 'hello' to some Russian soldiers was an invitation for rape, until the Russian Jewish officers put a stop to it. But before that a lot of the girls were raped, heartbroken, crying. Then a truck came from Waldenburg with men and women liberated a few days before us. I resembled my sister, and these people recognized me, so I knew my sister was alive in Waldenburg, but when I saw her I didn't recognize her. She had really gone through the horrors of the Holocaust. We went to Munich because we heard an uncle was alive there. It took days and days on trains, bribing guards with bottles of vodka, until we came to the American zone. There it was a different life, completely different. Freedom!"

WALTER SCHWARZ

TIMISOARA, ROMANIA

"It so happens my roommate was the leader of this group and he had some experience with Nazis. He urged all the Jewish students to leave: 'Get away from here as fast as you can, as far away as you can!'"

Walter Schwarz experienced the war years both as a victim of the Nazis before coming to the United States in 1940, as well as an interrogator of Nazi prisoners of war as a member of the United States Armed Forces.

Walter was born in Timisoara, Romania, an ethnically diverse area with Hungarian-, Romanian- and German-speaking people. He attended high school in his hometown but after graduation he was sent to Brno, Czechoslovakia, to train as a textile engineer so that he could follow his father's footsteps into that trade. His father also wanted him learn his native language, Czech. Walter became fluent in five languages. He spoke German at home, studied Hebrew at Hebrew school, and also spoke Hungarian, Romanian and Czech.

The school that Walter attended had a large Jewish population because the Jews of the area were very involved in the textile industry. On March 15, 1939, when the Nazis invaded Czechoslovakia, the cry *"Juden raus!"* ("Jews out!") echoed through his school halls. All the Jewish students were immediately evicted from the building.

"Where should I go?" Walter remembered thinking. "I went into the park, which was not far, and I saw all my friends gathered there and they were deciding what to do. It so happens my roommate was the leader of this group and he had some experience with Nazis. He had come from Germany and he went to my school. He urged all the Jewish students to leave: 'Get away from here as fast as you can, as far away as you can!'"

"For me 'far away' was Romania, which borders on Czechoslovakia, so that afternoon I bought a ticket at the railroad station. German soldiers and Nazis occupied all the important city offices, and the city hall and the telegraph and telephone office. And I had to get a permit from a German officer to buy a ticket.

"I talked to a German officer. I didn't tell him I was Jewish but I said my parents lived in Romania and I'd like to go home. So he didn't hesitate and he gave me — I think, maybe I didn't look Jewish —he gave me permission to leave, so I left." In Timisoara, Walter found his parents frantically trying to leave for the United States. Finally, in 1940, they were successful and left Romania by train for Genoa, Italy, where they boarded the last ship allowed to carry refugees to America before Italy joined the war against the Allies.

The U.S. military draft began immediately after the attack on Pearl Harbor in December of 1941, and Walter was drafted in March of 1942 at the age of 21. "I got into the U.S. Army and from then on I was chasing Nazis

Walter Schwarz

135

instead of being chased," he said. "My first assignment was a training camp at Camp Pickett, Virginia. At that time the Army was looking for people who spoke different languages. One day my commanding officer called me into his office and said, 'Pack your duffel bag. You're shipping out.'"

He was sent to Camp Ritchie, a Military Intelligence Training Center in Maryland. "In addition to English, everyone spoke at least German. Many of them spoke other languages, too." It was there that he became a member of the "Richie Boys," a special military intelligence unit comprised mainly of German-speaking immigrants, predominately Jewish, who had fled Nazi persecution. In addition to his training in basic military skills, Walter was trained to interrogate prisoners of war and learned to translate documents.

Walter was sent to England in September 1944 for more instruction, where he was stationed in Birmingham until he was sent to France in October 1944. He joined General Patton's Third Army and saw combat in the Saar region. In December 1944, he was involved in the Battle of the Bulge. "I ended the war in 1945. I happened to be stationed in Dresden, which is not far from Brno, where I started my life. But this time I was a hunter and the Nazis were being hunted."

LUCY SMITH

CRACOW, POLAND

"I am still in hiding, in a way. I could not go forward, even professionally, I couldn't exhibit my paintings. It took me a lot of time to learn to be open, to talk."

Lucy Kreisler was only six years old when the Germans occupied Cracow. Her father, a chemist and paint manufacturer, fled to Lvov, and Lucy and her mother went into hiding. Only when the war ended could she finally go to school.

"My mother did not give me much Judaism," said Smith. "I did not know there were Catholics and Jews or that I was Jewish. I knew there were holidays, and my uncle took me to temple a few times. I thought it was entertaining. I was supposed to start school the year the Germans came. I went for a month before I was told not to come any more. I also couldn't go to public parks anymore, but we went to the river and found places to play in the street.

"I did not have to wear a yellow star because I was under ten years old, but gradually it became more and more clear to me that I was Jewish. Some Poles occupied our apartment, and told my mother to get out. She couldn't take any furniture or anything.

"My mother came from a rather wealthy family. We went to Tarnow, where my mother was born, and stayed a year in a little apartment. The Germans were putting up posters telling Jews they needed to report. Her cousin told us not to trust the Germans, and not to do what they said, so she just didn't go. My mother had two uncles, almost her age, and the Germans came and shot both uncles in the street.

Lucy Smith

"We were always hiding. A Ukrainian was assigned by the Germans to administer our house in Tarnow. He was staying downstairs, and we were in the attic, and when the Germans would come he would say, 'No, nobody is upstairs.'

"Then we were in hiding in the ghetto. There was a cave for coal under the house, and a man covered up the door with bricks and left only a small passage underneath. One could just crawl through on one's belly, and then push a crate to cover the passage. There were maybe twenty of us hiding there, sometimes for several days, with just a little food.

"At the beginning in the ghetto we played on the balconies, and in the ruin of a synagogue next to our house. But the Germans would come to the ghetto and take anyone in sight, especially children and families with children, so there were fewer and fewer children. Finally, most of the children were gone.

"My father got false documents, Catholic certificates of baptism, for us. My mother got in touch with a gang that specialized in getting people out of the ghetto for money. There was a house with one side in the ghetto, and one outside the ghetto, on the border. The house was being used for delousing people, and we went there pretending we wanted to get deloused. Then these people opened the door, and we went through to the other side. The gang was waiting, and they took us to the train.

"We went to Warsaw because nobody knew us there, so it was less likely that someone would recognize us with our false identity. There was an apartment owned by a woman who was a part-time 'madame,' but there was a bed for us. We waited for our belongings, and eventually some clothes came, and a very precious thing for my mother—the down comforter. Mother had some rings which she sewed into her coat and sold from time to time. She also sold things from my uncle's store like combs. But part of living in hiding was paying blackmail, and the gang was always waiting to see how much they could squeeze out of us, after which they would denounce us.

"We found another place to live and didn't tell the gang. We lived there almost a year with the wife of a prisoner of war, a Polish officer, and her two daughters. They didn't know we were Jewish, but they also kept a man they knew was Jewish. When the ghetto burned, one daughter said, 'Let the Jews burn. Main Street used to be theirs!'

"When the Russians and Germans started fighting in Warsaw, we walked far away to Pruszkow, staying one night in a store where Polish women were so scared they were saying the 'Hail Mary' all night. This was fall 1944.

"My mother told a German officer we were Ukrainian and got permission for our group to go to Tarnow. It was absolutely quiet when we got there because no one was there. We went to our basement cave, and after a while we heard soldiers. Someone went out to check look, and there were not German soldiers but Russians! We all rushed out, and that was the end of hiding.

"Life started to be quite pleasant. Russians settled in the house where we lived, and they shared food with us, and I could go to school. Everybody was surprised to see people coming back after the war alive. My father didn't come back. On his way to Warsaw to bring those papers for us, there was sabotage at the train station by the Resistance and the Germans arrested everyone close to the station, including my father. My father died in Russia.

"After the war, I didn't think much about being a survivor. I felt terribly alone. I went to France by myself and studied art. In 1959 I married an American, and in 1967 we came to the United States."

JACK SUTIN

STOLPCE, POLAND

"Even if she had survived, the chances of her running into the same place in the woods where I was hiding were not even one in a million. But I believed in the dream . . ."

The story of Jack and Rochelle Sutin is like a fairy tale set amid the horrors of World War II, an improbable union of star-crossed lovers who defy the terror of war to find one another and survive.

The path that led Jack to Rochelle was like that of many Jewish youth growing up in Poland in the years preceding the war. Jack was raised in a moderately religious family in the Polish city of Mir. Like many of his friends, Jack belonged to a Zionist youth organization with the hope that he would eventually settle in Palestine. Also like many of his friends he faced constant anti-Semitism in school.

"I knew from the time I was two, three years old. By that age you knew that you were not the same as all the other kids," said Jack. "The teachers—and most of the students—in that school made things difficult for the minority of Jews who attended. We were singled out for special criticism, well beyond what a Polish student would receive. 'What's the matter, Jew?' the teacher would ask us. 'Can't you keep up?' During the recess, a small percentage of Polish students would be willing to include Jews in their game. Most would not."

By the time of Jack's bar mitzvah at age 13, he and several friends had made plans to attend an agricultural school in Palestine. Six months before the invasion of Poland their applications and deposits were sent in, but "the world was turned upside down and my papers never arrived," said Jack. He was trapped in Poland.

On September 1, 1939, Germany invaded Poland on the western front and the Russians invaded from the east. "We didn't hear about the atrocities in the western section of Poland for three or more months," said Jack. Even

Jack Sutin

though he lived in Russian-occupied eastern Poland, the residents soon began to learn about the confiscation of Jewish property, the imprisonment of Jews and the murders taking place in ghettos farther west. Life was hard under Russian domination but anti-Semitism as a policy, was forbidden.

The war with Germany did not reach the residents of far eastern Poland until June of 1941. As it became clear that the Nazi army would soon overtake the area, many people fled east in advance of the invasion in an attempt to reach Russia. Rather than flee to the east,

140

Jack left Stolpce, where he had been attending school, to be with his family in Mir. As liquidation of the Mir ghetto began, Jack and his father were hidden by Polish Christian families outside the village. His mother, who was considered an essential employee of the Reich, continued to work as a dentist in Mir until she was murdered by the Nazis. When the danger of hiding Jack was too great a risk for the Polish family protecting him, Jack returned to Mir. Soon he and the remaining Jews of the village were imprisoned in the ancient fortress of the Mir castle.

It was from this location that Jack and a group of men planned an escape to join Russian partisans in the nearby forest. "For those of us planning to escape, it was a horror to think of leaving family members behind," recalled Jack. "But there was, in our minds, no way of avoiding the conclusion that we would die whether we ran or stayed. And in that belief, we were proven right." Jack and his father were among the approximately 300 Jews who escaped from the Mir castle ghetto between August 9 and 10. The remaining Jews of the castle ghetto were murdered on August 14, 1942.

Jack and his father joined a group of Russian and Jewish partisans living in the woods. Survival was a process of hiding from the German and Polish police during daylight hours, scavenging for food at night and trying to stay alive during the harsh winter months. "We were doing our best to survive, even to resist, but no one in our group expected to come out alive from that hell," said Jack. "We were always armed and had an understanding that if we were ambushed, we would fight until we were killed. If it was inevitable that we would die, death would come on our terms." With the idea of inevitable death came a feeling of liberation. "I became extremely brave. I wasn't afraid of death any more. I established myself as the leader of the group and I took huge risks," said Jack.

Sometime in August or September of 1942, Jack had a powerful dream, a dream that he said he believed in completely, without logic or reason. In the dream Jack saw the face of Rochelle Schlieff. Jack first spotted Rochelle as a student in Stolpce and was immediately smitten although they never dated. Said Jack, "When I woke up I started to think, yes, I knew Rochelle before the war, but we didn't date or even have a close relationship. Why would she come into my dream? I didn't even know if she was still alive. And even if she had survived, the chances of her running into the same place in the woods where I was hiding were not even one in a million. But I believed in the dream…I took it so seriously that, while we were digging out our winter bunker—roughly a month after the dream—I insisted that we construct one extra space next to my own to be saved especially for Rochelle.

"When I told members of the group that Rochelle would be coming, they all thought I was going crazy. I didn't want to tell them about the dream. I didn't give them any explanation at all. I said only, 'Don't any of you worry about it. I just want a space ready for her when she comes.'"

In November 1942, the lookouts spotted a group of three Jewish women being led through the woods. They had instructions to speak to Izik (Jack) Sutin. "I had no idea who the women were—the guards hadn't gotten their names. So I went out to meet them. Rochelle was standing there. It was unbelievable! What I felt when I first saw Rochelle was that my dream had not lied to me. Someone, something, was watching over us. Rochelle and I had been fated to meet." That New's Year's Eve, with the partisans as guests, they married in the forest. "She'd lost her family, I lost my family. We took care of each other," said Jack.

Jack and Rochelle spent three years hiding with the partisans. They were liberated by the Russian army in the Nalibocka Forest. They returned to Stolpce and Mir but it was no longer a place where Jews were welcome. They eventually risked traveling to occupied Berlin and with the help of HIAS (Hebrew Immigrant Aide Society) and were sent to the Feldafing displaced persons camp, where their first child Cecilia was born. The family eventually emigrated to the United States in1949. Jack and Rochelle Sutin continued to take care of each other for 68 years of marriage until her death in 2010.

VICTOR VITAL

PATRA, GREECE

"I was a survivor in hiding. I was lucky not to be in the concentration camps and I owe that to my father who said when the Nazis came, 'We have to leave immediately.'"

"When I first came into the United States, I did not consider myself a survivor because I was not from the concentration camps, but for two years we had very difficult times," said Victor Vital. He and his family survived by hiding in the mountains of southern Greece.

Victor was born in Patra, Greece, a port city in southern Greece. It was an area held by the Italians and not directly threatened by German invasion until the pact between Italy and Germany collapsed and the Germans then occupied the entire county. "At that time, my mother's relatives and their families, about 90 people who lived in Salonika, were taken by the Germans to the concentration camps. None came out, none of these 90 people."

Word of the Salonika deportations quickly spread to the Vital family. "They sent us a notice to go away from the city and hide outside in the mountains, as

Victor Vital

far away as we could get, where no one would know us." Victor's father, Joseph, was president of the local Jewish community and well known in the town. It was through his friend, the police chief, that the family got new identification papers and began preparations to go into hiding. "We took whatever we could carry in our hands and in a small car and left. There were eight people in our group: myself, my father Joseph, my mother Rachel, my brother Marco, my sister Emily and her husband Nathan Asher and his parents Samuel and Regina Asher."

They left Patra in the early morning and spent the night in a small bombed-out church outside the city. From there they followed a path that would lead to the village of Vallatune. The trip took three days and nights. "At night we slept on the ground in fields, always fearful of snakes and wolves." They eventually settled in the cellars of two small houses where they kept a couple of goats. "We slept on the dirt floor of the cellars and we were infested with lice. A terrible thing—lice. We had to go into the forest to relieve our bowels—another terrible thing." Food for the families was scarce. "We went out in the field to gather greens. We bought cheese scrapings from the villagers. We bought wheat and ground it by hand to make bread. Our only beverage was water. We were always cold and hungry."

In November the family got word that there were Germans in the mountain villages looking for Jews. "So we had to go deeper in the mountains to another village. It took us two days and nights to travel there. Again we slept on the ground under the trees in the forest. We huddled together to try to stay warm but it was November and very cold. We would not even make a fire to warm ourselves or to cook what little food we had. We had to protect ourselves from the wolves, and if the Germans were close by, they would find out about us."

The situation became so desperate that Victor's father and brother-in-law decided to take a chance and go into the nearby village to seek help. When they reached a bombed-out church they met a Christian friend from their city who was also trying to find food for his family; it was a time of hunger and desperation for the entire Greek populace.

"He recognized my father and said, 'What are you doing here? Go back to the mountains. The Germans are looking for you and have put a reward out for you and your families.'" As the two men turned back to rejoin their families in hiding, the friend handed them a small bag of wheat. It was all he had. "I am here today, alive, because of the people who protected me."

"We could not have survived much longer under these conditions. Finally when the Nazis were defeated and left Greece, we returned to Patra. We were sick and hungry and we found that our home had been entirely destroyed. We had no furniture, dishes, cooking utensils or even running water. Our neighbors gave us what they could spare until my father found a job."

Victor Vital was twelve years old when his family went into hiding.

They returned to their home two years later. "The bad circumstances and the terrible life of those times are always in my mind. The suffering was beyond belief."

FELICIA WEINGARTEN

LODZ, POLAND

"In Bergen-Belsen we began to die. It was a slow process. One became thinner and thinner until one became a skeleton and died, either walking or sitting in the filthy barracks. I watched my mother dying."

Felicia Karo's father was a principal of a Jewish boys' high school. His family had lived in Poland since the sixteenth century. Felicia was thirteen years old when the war began.

"Before the war there was no ghetto and one was free to live almost anywhere," said Felicia. "I lived in a very nice residential area, where Jews were about 20 percent of the population. I used to play with Polish children, and my father would find jobs for our Polish neighbors.

"I was only a child, but you couldn't be Jewish then and not be concerned about what was happening to the Jews of Germany. In 1938 Jews who had been born in Poland but lived in Germany were forcibly thrown over the Polish border. The Nazis just rounded them up, and some of them came in robes and house slippers! When war broke out, we naively thought that maybe Poland would win. We were hoping England and France would come to the rescue. But Poland fell in less than two weeks.

"My father was arrested in October as a member of the Jewish intelligentsia. He came out of prison at the end of December and had to spend four weeks in a hospital to recover from the beatings and the lack of food in prison. In the meantime, we had been sent to the ghetto.

"My mother prepaid our rent for three months, actually a bribe so

145

Felicia Weingarten

we could keep a few sticks of furniture and some possessions. Our furniture was very big and very heavy, and we were not permitted to hire a wagon, so we took two small beds and dragged them on a sled, and left the rest where it was. For three of us we had a tiny little room, no bigger than a bathroom. There was no heating fuel, so we lived in 'ice palaces,' and we had to hack through ice to wash ourselves.

"On April 12, 1940, my fourteenth birthday, they put barbed wire around the ghetto and stationed armed guards around it. There were two sets of laws, one for Poles and one for Jews. The laws were in the newspapers and posted all over town. Curfew for Poles was 7 p.m., for Jews 5 p.m. Jews had to wear a yellow armband, later changed to a yellow Star of David on the left breast, on the back, and on our apartments. The German army was quartered in what had been the nicer Jewish apartments, and they helped themselves to Jewish goods. Little by little we were robbed of everything we owned.

"The Jews were highly skilled people in an industrial city, and they used us. Everybody from fourteen to fifty-five had to work twelve hours a day or night, in shifts. Then it became from age nine to sixty-five. And if one didn't work, one didn't get a ration card and was as good as dead. The food ration was cooked and issued at work. It was a little bit of bread, and 'soup' that was just lukewarm water, with maybe a bit of vegetable or potato floating in it. Very rarely were we issued a piece of meat, and almost never an egg or butter.

"We were ruled by the Judenrat, and we had Jewish bosses. If one had the right acquaintances, one could get a better job where there was a little

146

food or labor was not too difficult. At first I made decorations in a ladies' hat factory. Then I received a good job in a bakery, where I was given an extra bread ration. Later I worked in a kitchen, where I could eat a little and leave part of my ration for my parents. Then I worked in a laundry. The Nazis didn't know it, but I also secretly went to school —even in the ghetto!

"In the summer of 1944 there were about 70,000 of us still left, barely alive, in the ghetto. Parts of eastern Poland were under Russian control and we could hear the guns, but the Russians stopped their offensive which gave the S.S. time to liquidate the Lodz ghetto.

"In August and September 1944, from morning until late at night, soldiers, S.S., and special police went from house to house, flushing out whoever was hiding. Some people didn't try to hide because they were starving, and one received a loaf of bread if one went willingly. Some were caught right on the street. A classmate of mine didn't even have a chance to say goodbye to her mother. We were hiding in my father's office, but the office manager had a child who cried, and we were found.

"They took us to the depot. The German commandant responsible for the ghetto opened his coat and said, 'See, I have no guns. I've been your friend. We are going to resettle you to save you from the oncoming Russian Army.' We dreaded this so-called 'resettlement.' We knew that people who were sent away rarely came back, and sometimes a transport would stop and the people—skeletons—told of horrible beatings and torture and hunger. But we had absolutely no idea of concentration camps.

"They shoved us into cattle cars, and somebody found a piece of paper stuck between the slats, and he read it aloud. It said, 'Brothers, save yourselves. Death awaits you.' But it was too late.

"We went through the selection—life or death—men and women separately. It went very quickly. The German officers would, with the flicker of a finger, send you to the right or the left. I could see from the corner of my eye that to the right went women with children, sick people, grey-haired, cripples, or young women walking with middle-aged women. I was waved to the left. My mother was tall and beautiful with dark hair, and she, too, was waved to the left.

"We walked for miles to a bath installation. We were told to undress and line up, and give up our jewelry. I had a watch and a small diamond, my mother's engagement ring. I didn't want to give it to the S.S., so I threw it in a corner. They looked in our crevices, the mouth and elsewhere, to make sure we didn't hide jewelry or money. They cut our hair. Then they shoved us into a bath hall, and cold water came out. Then we stood naked, shivering, and after several hours they issued us striped uniforms or torn and ragged civilian clothing.

"We marched for several miles again to another part of the camp, and we were seated on the floor, packed like sardines. They made us open our knees and somebody would sit between your knees, until we formed fives. We got very tired from sitting in this position, and we started to complain and cry. Some young girls came running in and told us to stop. They said, 'This is a death camp.' I knew what death was, and I knew what a camp was, but I still recall trying to understand what these words meant together.

"There were constant beatings and 'selections,' weeding out those who were weak or emaciated, separating families, sisters, mothers, and daughters. On the fourth day, I found out that the ones they took went into the gas chambers.

"I stayed in Auschwitz only a week. Then there was a demand for Jewish labor, and we were sent to Germany to work in an airplane factory and then to a huge munitions factory in Bad-Kudova. German civilians lined up on the streets and made fun of us. They called us 'monkey people' and 'rag people' because we were wearing ragged dresses and our heads were shaved.

"The prisoners of war who worked in the factory, and the other slave laborers, who came from many parts of Nazi-occupied Europe, tried to cheer us up, and told us to hang on, that the Germans were losing the war. The foreman even came with a notebook and said to my mother, 'I'd appreciate very much if you would sign your name in this notebook and say I never hit you, that I treated you with as much humanity as I could.' And I realized that if a German foreman was that scared, the war must be close to an end.

"I remember only one act of decency from the S.S. Once an S.S. woman asked somebody, 'Did you have children?' And the woman said, 'Yes, I had a child who was taken away from me in Auschwitz.' The S.S. woman said, 'I would never give up my child.' The woman was afraid to say, 'I didn't give her up, she was taken from me.' She just cried, and the S.S. became very angry and made her work without a coat, and the woman was freezing. But about an hour later, another S.S. woman saw this poor woman's face, and her frozen fingers, and she removed her gloves and said to the woman, 'You can keep them.' Then she said very quietly, with tears in her eyes, 'I have a son fighting on the eastern front in Russia, and I hope perhaps somebody will be kind to him, too.'

"On the death march to Bergen-Belsen we walked through snow, away from the oncoming Russian army. I don't know how my mother survived those three days. I think love drove her. We could see blood on the snow, and she knew if she sat down, I would stay with her, and they would shoot both of us.

"In Bergen-Belsen, they did not distribute any food. There was very little drinking water, a lot of lice, no work. We began to die of disease and starvation. My mother and I became sick with typhus, burning up with fever. I had no water for my mother, and no medical care to save her.

"On April 15, 1945, I was freed by the British. Physicians came in wearing gas masks because we stank. Women were dying in their own excrement and lice. Mounds of bodies—among them my mother—were everywhere. Nobody had the strength to bury them. The British buried them with bulldozers. I was dying of malnutrition. I was so weak I could only walk a few steps. I could not speak above a whisper. I don't know how much longer I would have lived—a few days, a week.

"A-month-and-a-half after I was freed, a young army medical man said, to my amazement, 'Heart okay, lungs okay. You're okay.' I was still very thin, and my left leg would suddenly buckle under me and I'd fall, but I got a job with Jewish Relief because I knew Polish, German, Yiddish, enough English to fill out applications. I was nineteen years old.

"Survivors began to look for one another: friends, a brother or sister or a cousin, very rarely a parent or a child. My father had six brothers and a sister, all married with children. None survived. I visited the Jewish displaced persons camps where I found some friends and met my future husband.

"People began to marry, to make plans. Repatriation began for those who wanted to go back to wherever they came from. Illegal immigration began through Italy to Palestine. I came to the United States in April 1948. I learned to speak English better and got a job. My husband had been a medical student but he didn't know English, so he couldn't go back to medicine. It took a long time for me to process what I had lived through, My mother had believed in God very deeply and when I witnessed her death I wondered where God was. I pushed the thought of religion and God as far away as I could. But when my second son was born I went to the synagogue, and it reminded me of the synagogue in Lodz that my parents belonged to. I like being a Jew. Wherever I travel, I look up survivors who remember me as a child, who knew my parents. I am not a nobody to them."

LEO WEISS

DROHOBYCZ, POLAND

"When the Gestapo officer told us to get out, I said to him, 'I'm not going.' What? Telling a Gestapo officer that you're not listening to him?"

Leo Weiss was born in 1924, the son of a tailor. He grew up in the village of Drohobycz, Poland. Leo was sixteen years old when the Nazis invaded Poland.

"The minute the Nazis entered our city, the Jewish kids were not allowed to go to school," said Leo. The Nazis set up a ghetto in Drohobycz and all the Jews were required to live within its walls. "You couldn't get in and you couldn't get out unless you had a permit from the German authorities." After six months behind walls, the ghetto was liquidated. They took "the handicapped people, people that were really aged, sick children, little children, put them on the truck, took them outside of the city, told them to dig their own graves and killed them all."

Those who had the opportunity to survive were young and strong enough to work as slave laborers because the German army needed workers for the war effort, said Leo. He was lucky enough to be one of them. He worked for the Wehrmacht. The army issued him an identification number. "So long as I had that, I was alive. If I lost that they would take me away."

Although he and his family were separated at the liquidation of the ghetto, Leo always believed that his father had a hand in saving his life. When the concentration camp where Leo was imprisoned was liquidated, he remembered, all the young Jewish children were put into a Polish jail. "At some point, a Nazi officer comes in, one of the murderers, who we knew was capable of anything, called my name and my brother's name." Leo's initial thought was, "This is the end." But then he thought, "Perhaps maybe my father has a finger in it, in the sense he was a tailor and he sewed uniforms for the Gestapo, and they liked him because he was a good worker." He later learned that his father, knowing that the camp was being liquidated, had indeed asked the officer to spare the lives of his sons.

It was then that Leo committed an act of bravery which saved the life of a classmate. "If you had a chance to think about what you were going to do, you would never do it. It's a spontaneous act; something that just suddenly your brain reacts to. When the Gestapo officer told us to get out, I said to him, 'I'm not going.' What? Telling a Gestapo officer that you're not listening to him? At that particular point my life was already not worth that much because he could either use the stick to beat me to death or shoot me with his pistol. But he was intrigued. How did I dare say that? So he says, 'Why?' I said, 'Because I have a wife in there and I'm not going without my wife.' Leo wasn't married, but his schoolmate was in the next cell and he was trying to save her, too. Surprisingly, the officer let them both go.

Leo Weiss

Decades after immigrating to Canada, Leo's son Saul made a trip to Israel where he worked on a kibbutz. There he befriended a young English woman. Before returning to Canada, he stopped in London to visit his friend and meet her family. Upon meeting the girl's mother he introduced

151

himself as Saul Weiss She looked at him with astonishment. "I know this family," she said. Miraculously, the girl whose life Weiss had saved so many years before in Poland was the mother of the English girl that his son Saul met in Israel!

After the war Leo Weiss worked with the legendary Nazi hunter, Simon Wiesenthal. Although Leo remembered the terror he endured during the war, he was not looking for revenge against his captors. Rather it was his sense that justice needed to prevail for the millions who could no longer speak for themselves.

While all the members of his immediate family were separated during the war, they all survived and were reunited after liberation. When asked how he and his entire family managed to survive, Leo suggested that their survival was pure luck. But when asked how his grandfather managed to survive, Saul Weiss had a different answer: "It was his personal values that kept him alive during the Holocaust. My grandfather was a principled man who vehemently believed in specific values. His beliefs kept him going and that is why he survived such adversity."

"For many years I didn't want to talk about my experiences," said Leo, "but I realized that I need to do it for the kids." He has shared his story of survival with thousands of students in Canada and the United States. He usually began his presentation in the following way: "My name is Leo Weiss and I am a dinosaur. You know what happened to dinosaurs? They're extinct. My generation, Holocaust survivors, are on the verge of being extinct. . . . So it is vitally important for kids to learn about us."

FRED WILDAUER

RIGA, LATVIA

"Sometimes, in spring, I feel exactly that moment when I was liberated, how it was. In the middle of winter I sometimes walk outside at night and I'm alone and it's quiet and I am back in the ghetto, the wind blowing, the dreary, hopeless feeling, and then it comes to me—the memory of that night when I heard the shots, that night my family died."

On a single day in 1941, Fred Wildauer lost more than forty relatives. He and his younger brother survived because Fred's non-Jewish wife could bring them food to supplement their meager diet as slave laborers and because he was a mechanic, needed by the Nazis.

"My parents were Orthodox Jews," said Fred. "My father and mother sold ladies' and men's wear. They struggled to make a living. I only went to school until I was fourteen, and then I got my first full-time job as a mechanic in a knitting factory. Latvia was a very small country. There were 90,000 Jews, 40,000 of them in Riga, enough for two Jewish political parties, and enough Jewish votes to send a member to Parliament. When I was in the army, there came a directive from the war ministry that we should have the day off on Jewish holidays so we could attend religious services. But the commander was an anti-Semite, and he didn't follow the rule, so one of the Jewish soldiers wrote to a leader of one of the Jewish parties, and the commander was demoted. But a Jew could not rise to any rank above corporal. We never had a Jewish streetcar conductor or a Jew in the police force.

"After Hitler came to power in Germany, my father lost his business. They didn't let Jews have decent apartments. Jews could not get jobs. I can see myself right now, September 1939, sitting in a friend's apartment, I see the radio standing in the corner, and I hear the announcement that war has been declared.

"The Russians entered Latvia in June of 1940. They sent Germans back to Germany—people who had lived in Latvia for ten generations. All of a sudden, under the Russians, the doors were open to us, and Jews were equal to the rest of the population. Of course the Latvians resented this, and when the Germans marched in in 1941, the Latvians were very willing to help the Germans do what they did to the Jews.

"When Germany attacked Russia in June of 1941, we listened to war news from both sides. The Germans were reporting they had shot down fifty planes and lost one, and the Russians were reporting they had shot down fifty planes and lost one! My dad said, 'If I had a choice, I would rather take the Germans than the Russians.' But my sister said, 'You don't know what you're talking about!' I still remember the way she said that.

"The German army was fighting the Russians, so Latvian collaborators formed 'freedom fighter' units with bright white and red armbands. The very first night, they came to our house because we lived about half a block away from the big building which had been the Latvian ministry of the interior.

"They knocked on every door and took all the Jews of out of our apartment building, about twenty-five of us. We were taken to the headquarters building, where there were several Latvians and a high-ranking German officer. The toilets were overflowing, and they made us clean up the mess. We then swept the yard, and my older brother swept and swept, and swept himself out the gate, and walked away. I followed him and my younger brother followed me, the same way.

"The next morning I headed for the factory where I worked. My boss, a Jew, was replaced with a Latvian manager, but he got me a pass to go to work and not be arrested. We had to register. We had the word 'Jew' stamped into our passports. We were given yellow stars, and we had to wear them on the chest and the back of our clothes. We were only allowed to shop in a Jewish area, so we had to walk across the city to buy groceries, and people would spit on us as we walked by.

"They fenced in part of the city and told the Jewish committee to allot two square meters per person. Two or three families lived in one room with a curtain across. I bluffed my way into a little milk store and moved in there, together with my younger brother and my sister and her two children. My parents found one room and a kitchen. They had five rooms of furniture, and the furniture remained in the yard. Every morning they would go down and break up a piece of furniture and use it for kindling wood.

"November 29, 1941, there were placards all over saying that the ghetto was going to be moved, and everybody was allowed to take twenty pounds along. Everybody put on the most valuable things they owned. If they had diamonds or money or gold buried in the ground, they dug it up and sewed it into their clothes to take along. People who worked in town, like we did, were not allowed to go back to our families, and we ended up nine men in one tiny room.

"In the middle of the night I heard shots. I thought they came from the town, maybe an uprising of Latvians against the Germans. I didn't realize Latvian guards were taking the Jews out of the ghetto in groups, into the woods. Later we heard that Russian prisoners had dug trenches, and the Jews had been made to take off, in orderly German fashion, their shoes, their coats, their glasses, whatever they had on. In their underwear they were made to go into those trenches and were shot. Meanwhile, the Germans were ripping the clothing apart, looking for valuables.

"That night I lost almost everybody in my family—my parents, my two sisters, their children, aunts, uncles, cousins. The Germans were clever about it. They couldn't get everybody out the first night, so to prevent people from running, letters came to the ghetto a day later, saying, 'We are all well. The quarters are better here,' and listing twenty or thirty names. Everybody found a name that could be an uncle or a friend. But there were 24,000 people, so twenty names was nothing! My wife came to see me at the university where I worked. Dressed like a student, she walked through the halls—and that was the first time I broke down and cried.

"There were six of us who worked at the university as handymen. We fixed cars, bicycles, motorcycles, the electricity. The Germans got tired of hauling us back and forth, so they gave us a room, formerly a theater, and said, 'Build yourselves some bunks.' My shoes wore out, so they took us to a clothing store and told me I could pick out my own pair of shoes. At night they told us to lock ourselves in. They had a theory, 'My Jews are good Jews.' We could have walked away and nobody would have known it for a while, but where could we have gone? Two of my friends just walked one day away, and somebody hid them for a couple of years, and both of them survived.

"In late summer of 1943, our unit was sent to a camp outside Riga. There were a couple of thousand people there, people who were not even Jews— German communists and criminals, even a murderer. We slept on boards, no straw, nothing. Again I was lucky. When I had been at the university, I was working on a delousing unit and it needed water, so they put it next to the kitchen. The cook and the stoker asked if I could get them some tobacco. My brother was working on a farm and he always brought back tobacco leaves and dried them in the barn, so I brought a bunch of those leaves to the cook and the stoker. Now, here in the camp, was that cook again, and he said, 'If you need anything, come to the kitchen.' To have a right to walk into the kitchen in a concentration camp is like having a ticket to the White House! So every morning I went to the cook, and it was like shopping in a grocery store. I would pick up potatoes and peas and chunks of horsemeat, and I gave food to my brother.

"Then the cook said, 'You're going out with Umbrey.' Umbrey was the

155

stoker, the other guy who got the tobacco from me! We went out every day, several hundred prisoners, to work on gasoline storage tanks, putting a cement wall around each tank so if one blew up, they wouldn't all go. It was so cold, we tied rags around our feet to try to keep warm.

"Luckily, I was only in that camp for six weeks. They took us to Stutthof, a big camp—45,000 people subdivided into little camps with different treatment. There was a German submarine commander, and the whole Lithuanian government, even a Danish police force! The barracks for Jews were designed for 300 people, but they took in 1,500.

"In the middle of the night a guard turned on the lights and ordered us to line up outside, and we had to run a gauntlet with Polish guards standing with big sticks and planks, hitting everybody who came out. Then we had to run back. This whole process was repeated three or four times that night. I was lucky. I got a knock on the shoulder, but many people were walking around with bloody heads and broken bones.

"I saw for the first time a crematorium. Every day they took groups of people, maybe ten or twelve, mostly women. The people knew where they were going, you could see it on their faces and by the way they were walking. The smell was always hanging over that area.

"It was foggy and wet, and to keep warm we would build 'furnaces.' Five or six guys would stand in a circle, calling other guys to stand behind them, and pretty soon it would be like a huge beehive, hundreds of people standing in one mass, and inside was warm. Sometimes we would sing and start to sway, and we could stand for hours and hours that way.

"They had a little narrow track railroad where they brought in potatoes. We had to dump the cars, put them back on the tracks, push the train out, then put the potatoes in boxes and run across the road to a field where we buried the potatoes for winter. I used to eat raw potatoes like an apple. The whole German population from the town walked by us when they went to the railroad station, so if there's anybody who says they didn't know there was a concentration camp, they are liars!

"My older brother didn't survive Stutthof. One night they took everybody out of his barracks and gassed them on the road in those infamous trucks.

"We were put on a train to Magdeburg. The last four or five months were pitiful sight. Many people died. Hunger can do terrible things. I found a big can where they dumped food for the dog, and the dog could only reach part way into the can. There was mold in there, but we cut it out with a knife, pulled out a couple of dog hairs, had a Sunday dinner.

"On April 12, 1945 we were working on the outskirts of the city when an American tank went by. Our guards took off, and we were free, but we didn't have any place to go. So we went back to the camp, found something to eat, and my brother and I lay down to sleep in the S.S. guards' quarters. In the middle of the night an announcement on the loudspeaker woke us up. The American tanks had pulled back, some of the guards came back to the camp, and we dumbbells were sitting in the camp! It was pitch black night and my brother and I pulled a couple of boards out of the fence, which made a terrible noise, but I stuck my shoulder through, and I was outside! My brother followed me, and in about five minutes the rest of the guys were out, too.

"We started to walk toward where we thought the American lines were. We were in the bombed-out area of the city, and we climbed over the rubble and found a basement. The building had been blown away by a bomb, but the basement was three compartments. One must have belonged to a painter, there were supplies and ladders. The next one just had empty crates. But the third one had everything that a guy on the run could want! Canned food, asparagus, carrots, potatoes, matches, furniture. I made myself a bed in a huge wicker basket and my brother slept on a loveseat.

"There was a German civilian there, afraid the Americans would kill all the Germans, so every day for seven days he brought us a bucket of water, sometimes a piece of bread. Then one day he didn't show up. I heard a lot of noise and I looked, and there was an American soldier standing by a truck. He wore a plain green uniform, and he looked like a gentile, but he said to me in Yiddish, 'Are you Jewish?' I said 'Yes,' and he said, 'Me, too.' The first American soldier we saw! It was April 20, 1945—a beautiful day.

"I wanted to find my wife. We had agreed that in case we survived the war we would write to a lady we knew on the west bank of the Rhine River. My brother and I waited for an answer, but then we decided not to wait any longer. We walked across Germany to get to that little village and found the lady had died!

"The people there said they thought my wife had gone to Solingen. I couldn't find her there, but on the way out of town we saw a little printing store with a sheet of paper in the window. I went in and said, 'I would like to put out a search ad.' I wrote down my wife's name, Tamara Lilget, and the man said, 'I know her, she lives in the next street.' And there I found my wife!

"I wanted to go to the United States so I wrote to the soldier who liberated me. His mother had promised herself that if her son came back from the war unharmed, she would do something for somebody, so she sponsored us."

DORA ZAIDENWEBER

RADOM, POLAND

"The thought of death was with me for so long that it no longer scared me. All the emotion left in me was regret-sorrow that I, too, would end up on a pile of bodies, discarded like so much trash."

Dora Eiger's father was a community leader, a member of the executive committee of Poland's Zionist Labor Party. Dora was only fifteen when the Germans took Poland. At nineteen, she married Jules Zaidenweber in the Radom forced labor camp, where both were prisoners.

"Radom was a town of 100,000, about 25 percent Jewish," said Dora. "It was a vibrant, active Jewish community. After World War I my father was planning on going to Palestine, but his father died and he was the oldest son, so he went to school and became an accountant. We had a large, very beautiful apartment, and my mother was an elegant lady. We were in school six days a week. We had an awful lot of homework, but we had no television to distract us. We belonged to youth groups, went skating in winter, and played tennis in summer. I was a gymnast and in track.

"If a Jew insulted a Pole, he could be taken to court and severely punished for it, and there were young thugs who belonged to an organization which was violently anti-Semitic. But a neighbor girl might say to me, 'You Christ killer!' and then ten minutes later, she'd come back and say, 'You want to play?' So we didn't live our lives terrified all the time. Hitler was in Germany and we were in a different country, and it seemed that we lived in a civilized world.

"When war broke out, I would look up and seeing the anti-aircraft fire, the little silver bullets. German planes came in so low we could see the faces of the pilots, and the planes were spraying the area with machine gun fire. This is something we saw in the movies, but we never thought it would happen to us.

"One week later, the Germans marched into town. A lot of orders were posted on walls. Everybody had to register to get an identification card and a ration card. Jewish I.D. cards were blue, and had the word 'Jew' stamped on them. We had to start wearing an armband with the Star of David, which identified us as Jews. German soldiers could just come into our apartments and take furniture, linens, and silver, and send it home. We had German officers billeted in our apartment, so we had to be very quiet, very careful what we were saying and doing. We had a live-in maid, but the German did not allow the maid to clean his room. I had to clean it.

Dora Zaidenweber

"To make a living, one either bartered or worked for the Germans. Radom was in Poland's 'Iron Triangle,' with a very large weapons factory and other munitions factories in neighboring towns. Another big industry was leather tanning. The Germans were in great need of leather, and they had to keep the people who knew how to mix the chemicals for tanning. These factories may be the reason why there are many more survivors from Radom, percentage-wise, than from other cities.

"The tanneries were my father's clients, and accounting still had to be done, so my father was working and was actually earning money. But there was a lot of poverty, a lot of sickness. The Jewish community had soup kitchens, and a lot of people wanted to put their children in the Jewish orphans' home, so the children would at least have some food.

"The beginning of 1941 all Jews had to move into two ghettos, in areas of tenements and very poor-quality houses. Because my father was who he was, we and our neighbors got a house that had four rooms. It had an outhouse, and the water pump outside, but each family had one room, so it was really terrific compared to where people lived two and three families in one room. That's when I met Jules, my husband, because his family moved next door. That summer our romance started blooming.

"In June of 1941 the Allies had to run for their lives to England and the Germans sent the Russians running. We started developing a nihilistic attitude, sort of 'to hell with it all,' trying to live every day to the fullest because it looked like there wasn't much left of our youth. There was a curfew in the ghetto. You couldn't go out after eight o'clock, but we sneaked through backyards, and we partied and did a lot of laughing and talking and joking. Since schools were closed, groups of us met with teachers and continued with our classes, which was very dangerous.

"On April 28, 1942, the knock on the door came at our house. A Gestapo man with a list in his hand asked if Isaiah Eiger lived in this house. My father hugged us and walked out with the Gestapo. We were just rudderless, floating. We had lost our protector. But then my mother gathered herself together, started making decisions. She had to feed us, so she started trading on the black market. A Polish woman who had been my uncle's housekeeper would purchase food, bring it to the wooden wall surrounding the ghetto, take money from my mother, and hand her the bundle. Then my mother would keep some for us and sell the rest to other people, making enough money to buy more.

"On August 6 the Germans emptied out the small ghetto in Radom and they brought to our ghetto with and rounded up another 2,000 people. They didn't get to us, but our whole family was gone, grandmother, great-grandmother, all the aunts, uncles, cousins. We didn't know what happened to the people in the boxcars. The word 'gas chamber' hadn't surfaced yet.

"Those remaining were put to work as slave labor. Now we were six people in a tiny little room, maybe nine by fifteen, just filled with beds. The Germans staged raids in the daytime to flush out those who weren't at work. Twice they lined up people and just counted ten, and executed every tenth person. I was weeding a huge field of lettuce and radishes and other vegetables twelve hours a day, and a soldier with a gun was standing there watching. I was assigned to mend rugs. I made covers for mattresses. I was a maid, a cook who didn't even know how to boil water. I did clean-up work after painters.

"Jules and I got married on July 8, 1943. That was some kind of a wedding! The Jewish head of the labor camp was empowered to perform marriages, and Jules saved that marriage certificate by hiding it in his shoe.

"We were sent to work at the weapons factory. I was in a women's barracks and Jules was in a men's barracks. I was the finisher, the polisher, in the woodworking shop. We were supposed to be making shipping boxes for guns, but a lot of Germans had us make fancy furniture for them. They would take the furniture to their home and bring me there to finish it. I could have walked out and just disappeared, but a friend of mine walked away, and her father was tortured to death.

"One hot July day in 1944, we were marched out, 2,000 people guarded by S.S. with machine guns and dogs. A young boy tried to escape and they made him kneel in front of everybody and they shot him point-blank with a handgun. If people lagged behind, we heard the shots. As the guards saw people who had a hard time walking, they invited them to get on horse-drawn wagons following us, and soon the wagons came back empty. It was a trail of blood and bodies.

"The end of the third day, we arrived at Tomaszow and the women were taken to the local jail. We had no water, not much food, no toilets. After a week there, we were marched to railroad tracks, and there were the men! We cried, we embraced, and then we were separated again, and put in cattle boxcars. This looked like absolutely the end.

"Sunday morning we arrived. The sky was as blue as can be. The sun was shining. As they opened the boxcars we saw the sign, 'Arbeit Macht Frei.'

'Where are we?' we asked. And somebody said, 'Auschwitz.' Nobody needed to tell us what was going on in Auschwitz. The smell told us all, the horrible smell of burning human flesh. They were shouting orders. 'Get undressed! Line up!' They were shaving off people's hair. The whole situation was totally unreal, we were laughing, crying and laughing.

"They told us to take our shoes with us. We were lucky because my mother had red shoes with heavy heels, and she had diamonds hidden in those heels, which later came in very, very handy.

"One German officer was very tall, extremely handsome, wearing a monocle. He had a little stick under his arm, and he was wearing white gloves. There he stood, one finger pointing to the right or to the left. Those who were young and still in good shape were on one side. On the other side were women whose bodies were older, the skin hanging. The officer was Dr. Mengele. Our group was shoved into a room that had shower heads. Water came out. Later I found out that the gas chamber on the other side also had shower heads. When we came out they handed us a dress, that's all.

"Even in Auschwitz people settled down to a certain routine. There was always the chance that you'd get sick, that they would pick you for medical experiments, but in the meantime you had a routine to feel that you're still a human being. You'd think, 'What's the use?' And you had to say, 'I'm fighting. I resolve to be alive.'

"I was assigned to a sewing workshop, where I secretly made aprons and blouses for women who worked in the kitchen, to wear under the scratchy prison uniform. In return they gave me margarine, sugar, marmalade. We had come to Auschwitz in August. In November the whole extermination process stopped. Transports were no longer arriving, they were leaving. In January the Germans blew up the crematoria and the gas chambers, and on the 18th of January we were marched out, thousands of women, in the snow.

"In the three days on the march, we stopped in villages, where we were put up in barns. On one occasion, the people let some of us into their houses. Inside a warm house, can you imagine! And they gave us hot soup! On the third day we were put in open boxcars. When the train stopped at Grossrosen, I impulsively said to one of the guards, 'Could I get a drink of water?' He just kept walking, but later he came back and handed me a canteen of warm water with a slice of bread floating in it! It sort of restores your belief that some human beings are decent.

"Next the train stopped in Buchenwald, where we were crowded into closed boxcars. For four days the train moved and stopped, and moved and stopped. We got off in surroundings that were breathtakingly beautiful, a forest of pines with snow on the branches. There was a moon. We were marching again, and finally we came to a barbed wire fence and barracks with signs in French, Italian, and Russian. It was an empty prisoner of war camp. We were the first inhabitants of Bergen-Belsen, one of the most infamous of the end-of-the-war camps.

"Daily, thousands of people were arriving. Each day we were given a slice of bread and a cup of soup made of rutabagas and water. Then the bread was cut out. Once I had some potato peels to eat, and I really just relished that marvelous food. Lice appeared in the straw we slept on, and people were dying of typhus.

"By the end of March, only eight weeks since we arrived, half the 35,000 prisoners were dead of starvation or disease. I became very, very sick with typhus. I tried to pretend I wasn't sick, to go to roll-call every day, but one day I just folded, and they took me to the 'hospital' to die. My mother still had the diamonds in her shoes, and she went to the woman in charge, and that's where one diamond ring went. That's how I came out alive from that death-trap 'hospital.'

"On April 15, 1945, the sun was shining on this indescribably horrible hell of a camp. We were shadowy skeletons. We heard rumors that Allied forces were on German soil, but when I heard a commotion, I didn't even raise my head. Then I heard a voice coming over the loudspeaker, not in German but in Polish, the most beautiful words, 'We have come to free you. This is the Polish Brigade of the British Army.'

"They gave us freshly baked bread and soup with pieces of meat and fat in it. Some people actually died from eating it! Then they started giving us very bland, cereal-type food, what our stomachs could tolerate. I weighed about fifty pounds when I was liberated. In three months I doubled my weight.

"UNRRA officials asked us to decide where we wanted to go. Mother was with me, but we didn't know if anybody else was alive. Then one morning in July I was walking to town, and I saw a figure in the distance.

"The step looked familiar. It was Jules! Jules and my brother, David, were liberated together, and my father was liberated in Theresienstadt by the

Russians. We were so fortunate!

"Jules and I started making our way to Heidelberg, where some Radomers were. The Americans put us in a castle, incredibly beautiful. Then our whole group was transported to Stuttgart and put in apartments which had been cleared of Germans.

"We'd lost five years. Jules wanted to study electrical engineering, so I started working for UNRRA because somebody had to earn money. We didn't have to pay rent or buy food, and the Joint Distribution Committee sent us used clothing, but to go to a theater or restaurant occasionally, you had to have some money.

"Then in 1948 we decided that I needed an education, too. I was the only Jewish person in the department of economics, out of some 200 students, but I spoke German fluently, so they didn't know I was Jewish until summer, when they saw the number tattooed on my arm. Then the young men, all Germans, immediately started telling me that they had fought in France, Belgium, Holland, Norway. Funny how nobody had been in Poland!

"Jules's mother went to Israel, and we really wanted to go to Israel, too. But my mother died, and my father and David left for the United States, and suddenly I realized that if I went to Israel, I might never see my father and David again.

"The first winter in Minneapolis in 1950, I thought I was in Siberia! I got a job and was admitted to graduate school in economics at the university. People reached out in certain ways, but they had relatives, friends already. Our social activities were among ourselves. Also, nobody wanted to talk about the Holocaust, and we had a real need to talk about it, to bear witness.

"Some say, 'Why not just forget it and live a normal life?' There is no normal life after the Holocaust. I speak to students and adult groups about the Holocaust, about people who would treat other human beings, how any group can be victimized, how the rest of the world turned away and pretended it wasn't happening. They didn't want to get involved. And therein is really the lesson of the Holocaust.

"The question of resistance often comes up because Americans' notion of heroism always has to do with resistance, with fighting back. I point out that there was armed resistance in many ghettos and camps, but those who carried it out invariably died. Simple survival in those extermination camps was an act of resistance, every minute."

SABINA ZIMERING

PIOTRKOW, POLAND

"A Holocaust starts or stops with a single human being. I was nineteen years old, and I said, 'I don't want to let the Germans kill me. I don't want to die. Not now!'"

Sara Szwarc (Schwartz) was sixteen when war began. She and her sister, Helena, survived because they looked and acted like Poles and because two of their Catholic schoolmates became members of the Polish Cap Underground.

"I grew up in Piotrkow-Tryb, 100 miles southwest of Warsaw," said Sabina. "In a population of about 60,000 people, 12,000 were Jews. We lived in a Polish neighborhood. We celebrated all the Jewish holidays, but I grew up with Polish friends and went to a Polish school. My Polish was accent-free, and I was very familiar with Polish customs and religion. My Polish friends would say, 'Oh, you're such a fun kid! Why don't you come with me to church and convert!' I told my mom, and she laughed. But growing up this way gave me the confidence to pass as a Pole during the war.

Sabina and Rubin Zimering

165

"For weeks before war broke out, we had to practice covering the windows in case of bombing attacks. September 1, 1939, a beautiful Friday morning, I went with my mother to a farmer's market. We heard the siren, but we all assumed it was another drill. A few minutes after that, bombs were falling. I was sixteen and I remember thinking that our sleepy town will finally have some excitement!

"Our family tried to escape to the East. German planes were machine-gunning people on the ground, so we hid in the woods in the daytime and walked at night. In a whole week we made in only thirty miles, so we went back home. A month later, Piotrkow had the first Jewish ghetto in German-occupied Poland. Our family of five was put into one room with another family. You could hear the heavy boots of patrolling soldiers from blocks away, always two and three together. Food was rationed and very scarce, and people began dying of hunger and typhus.

"The Germans turned over most of the job of running the ghetto to the Jewish Council. The ghetto was beautifully run, food distributed, sick people put in quarantine for typhus or sent to the hospital, but it was not an easy job for the Judenrat.

"In spite of constant fear and hunger, we still lived like seventeen-year-olds. We had an eight o'clock curfew, but we would meet in the small backyard of our apartment building with other teenagers, new boys from Lodz whose families were forced to leave their city. We had a group of maybe fifteen or twenty young people, a literary club. One of our leaders said, 'Why don't we resist?' This was such a surprising thought, and we were shocked.

"My Jewish high school was closed right away, as were Jewish grade schools. Jews were not allowed to congregate in groups of more than five or six, but education continued illegally. I was teaching children in their homes, and my friends and I continued our studies with Jewish professors.

"The adults spent the evenings pondering the future, but whenever the discussion turned to approaching disaster such as rumors about the liquidation of our ghetto, my grandfather vehemently protested, claiming that God would not allow this to happen. I did not contradict my grandfather, but I did believe rumors that the Germans systematically were exterminating one ghetto after another and that our turn was coming.

"I felt an inner revolt. My parents were saying, 'What will happen to others, will happen to us. Don't bother us.' But I did continue to bother, and finally my mother had an idea. She contacted our Catholic childhood friends, two sisters whose mother had been my grade school teacher, and asked if one of them could give me her passport. They said they would have to discuss it with their mother.

"The punishment for Poles helping Jews was death. But a few days later our friends came and said, 'Pick Polish-sounding names. Get photographs. We will give you passports.' I remember the expression on my parents' faces. A miracle! On October 20, 1942, shortly before midnight, the passports were put to use. Liquidation commandos surrounded the ghetto, and we could hear shots and screams. We took off our Star of David armbands and went into the scary outside world.

"At first our friends hid us in their attic. We couldn't move, we couldn't cough, because the father was against hiding us. But when he went to work, we could come down and eat and talk. Out of 20,000 Jews in the ghetto, the Nazis kept 2,000 for work, our father and brother among them. Our mother was sent with the rest to Treblinka. Our father told us to go to the next town and sign up to work in Germany, where it would be easier for us to pass as Poles.

"Now, for the first time in our lives, my sister and I had to rely only on ourselves. I was nineteen and she was seventeen. It seemed safer to pretend we were cousins, so I was Krystyna Slawinska and she was Helena Kowalska. We ended up working in a road machinery factory in Neustadt-Orla, with hundreds of women from all over Europe. With each new transport, we could see girls who looked just like us—not Polish, but Jewish.

"Once in a while some German soldier seemed decent, not comfortable with what he was doing. Some of the German workers invited us to their homes, gave us clothes, food, shoes. But there were remarks about our resemblance to each other, and we decided to run again. On a Friday evening we slipped out of camp and walked to town, where we were promptly arrested. Our camp director vouched for us, that we'd never done anything wrong before, but back at the camp one woman told us, 'They suspect you are Jews. Don't stay.' So we took off again, this time on a train heading south.

"My plan was to cross into Switzerland, but our money ran out. We ended up in Regensburg, north of Munich. We found an employment office and applied for work, pretending we had been accidentally separated from our transport. We were told to go to the next building, where they might help us find our lost group. The next building turned out to be Gestapo headquarters! We were subjected to a body search. They found a ration card for soap, with the name and address of our factory, but I quickly collected my wits, and said a Polish girl in Leipzig gave us this coupon. We were allowed to return to the employment office, where they were quite surprised to see us back.

"We spent the next eighteen months in Regensburg, worrying constantly about being recognized, working in the Maximilian Hotel, which served military dignitaries. By April of 1945 the city was being shelled by heavy artillery. Retreating soldiers were sleeping in doorways, everywhere, some wounded. It was obvious the German army was collapsing. Concentration camp Jews were brought to clean up from the shelling, and every day when the prisoners came, I looked in hope that I would see my father.

"April 27 a very, very unusual quiet came over the city. People started to come out of basements where they were hiding, and then trucks full of American soldiers came driving through the city. They were whistling at us girls and shouting 'Hitler kaput!' and throwing cigarettes and candy. The Americans looked like kids. They had soft-soled boots, and when they walked, you couldn't hear them. It was not like the Germans, with the stomping boots. The Americans walked like civilians!

"Our Polish friends' mother was in a concentration camp for smuggling information and weapons between Underground groups. The older sister was in jail, about to be executed, when the war ended. To show my appreciation for the risk they took for us, I sent packages and medicine and brought them to America in 1979 to visit. They were honored at my synagogue, and I also contacted Yad Vashem to recognize them as Righteous Gentiles."

Sabina Schwartz Zimering "passed" as a Catholic and worked as a maid at the Hotel Maximilian in Regensburg, Germany, from 1943 to 1945. After the war in Europe ended May 8, 1945, Sabina helped teenage concentration camp survivors search for surviving family members.

THE LIBERATORS

The term "liberator" is most often applied to the American soldiers who were the first to arrive at the barbed-wire enclosures surrounding Ohrdruf, Buchenwald, Dachau, Mauthausen, and other concentration camps. It was springtime, April and May of 1945, and World War II was coming to an end. American soldiers had read about German atrocities in their military newspaper, "Stars and Stripes." But nothing they read had prepared them for the immense and intensely human dimension of what they found—the smells, the emaciated bodies stacked like firewood, and the survivors, many of whom looked like walking skeletons. One liberator said, "Only their eyes were human size."

Here are the stories of some liberators. They, too, are witnesses to the Holocaust.

RICHARD DARR

WITNESS TO THE LIBERATION OF OHRDRUF AND BUCHENWALD

"It was a total shock, to see people who had been treated like this. I don't think there are any words that can truly express the impression it made on me. I—I can't. It's just impossible."

Richard Darr was drafted in September 1942. As a squad leader in the 260th Infantry Regiment, he saw active combat in Holland, Luxemburg, Germany, and Austria. After the war he worked in Germany for the American occupation forces.

"Our unit began in combat during the assault on Metz," said Richard, "and we continued east, engaging in spasmodic contact with the enemy. The war was beginning to draw to an end, and German prisoners were coming in in droves. When we arrived at Ohrdruf labor camp, and then Buchenwald, the guards had left. The prisoners there knew we were defeating the Germans, hat we were coming, and they were hanging on the barbed wire fences to greet us.

"These camps were an unbelievable, shocking sight. The living looked like cadavers, and in the open burial pit dead people were stacked, literally stacked, like cordwood.

"The buildings were one-story wooden structures, narrow but quite long. Inside, bunks were five or maybe six high, no headroom, so people in them couldn't sit up. The people crammed in there were too weak to get out, physically incapable of standing up and greeting us. Some could just hold out their hands.

"We spent the night sleeping on the ground outside the barbed wire. We were told not to mingle in the camp because of the danger of getting typhus, but some of us went in. Some prisoners could speak fairly good English, and I'd had two years of German in college.

"We gave them everything we had, too much. We had K-rations in boxes about the size of a Crackerjack box. Supper would be powdered drink mix, a can of deviled ham, crackers, maybe a chocolate bar and five cigarettes. Breakfast was canned eggs and powdered coffee, powdered milk. But if a survivor got chocolate bars from twenty troopers and had been virtually starved for months—well, he could become very ill.

"I returned to Germany in 1948. I was on the three-man economic advisory staff to General Clay, and then I was military governor in Baden-Wurtemberg. We wore a sport coat or a business suit to the office. That was part of the de-Nazification program, wearing civilian clothes to re-educate the German populace to democracy.

"There was a small Jewish displaced persons camp in my area, and one day German policemen arrested a resident of the camp for selling black market meat. There was plenty of proof that Jews wouldn't have gotten a fair trial in a German court, so I asked the German policemen, 'Do they raise cattle in the displaced persons camp?' Obviously they didn't raise cattle. Then I told the police, 'Well, you will have to bring me the German farmer who sold the black market meat to the displaced persons camp inmate.' With that, the German police dropped the case!"

DONALD DEAN

WITNESS TO THE LIBERATION OF MAUTHAUSEN

"I still have some file sheets I took from the camp office. Typed lists, one line for each prisoner. Nationality, last name, first name, date of birth, date of death, and the running total of how many people had died up to that moment. The last number on the sheets was 21,388. And somebody was typing on those lists every day, keeping track."

Donald Dean graduated high school in 1929, the beginning of the Depression. He enlisted in the army in 1942.

"I was a warrant officer in ordnance," said Donald. "We repaired tanks that were shot up, other vehicles, field artillery, controlled all the repair parts—engines, axles, transmissions. We had forty trucks loaded with parts that moved into combat with the troops.

Survivors at Mauthausen, Austria, June, 1945
Photo by Donald Dean

"At Linz, Austria, word came that there was a concentration camp about fifteen miles south, so another fellow and I drove down there. As we got closer to Mauthausen there were inmates who had been liberated the day before. Most were so exhausted by the time they got across the road, they had to lay down to rest! One guy had gotten a machine gun, and he was having the best time. They'd find S.S. troopers who had worked in the camp and kill them right then and there. One German fellow, who had worked where they hung and shot prisoners, was lying there with a rake through his skull.

"The commanding officer of the unit occupying the camp put out a Proclamation that civilians in the towns of Mauthausen and Diessen would dispose of the bodies. The Germans came in vests and fedora hats to help bury these people. There was a big ditch, a mass grave, and they'd pick the bodies up unceremoniously by the arms and legs, lay them on a wheelbarrow, push them over and lie them down in the graves. The stench was terrible.

"We saw a big door that looked like a walk-in cooler. We opened it and there was a room, I'd say twenty by twenty feet. In the ceiling were showerheads which actually were gas heads. The floor level was about three feet down below the level we were at, and this room was completely full of bodies, full three feet deep. They'd kill them—the gas would put them away pretty fast, although some said the screaming and hollering was terrible—and then they'd put them into the ovens. The ovens were still warm when we got there, full of ashes.

"Inside one building I saw the most gruesome thing. They'd taken bunk beds, three high, and pushed them all together so they actually were shelves. It was dark in there and it was wet, just dripping wet, and inside were people who had been so mistreated they were crawling around, just insane, and in such misery.

"The fellow, a former prisoner, who showed us around, spoke pretty good English, and he told us how they caught him eating a raw potato he'd stolen out of the kitchen. They stood him up on a foot stool, put a rope through an eyebolt up in the ceiling, then they tied his hands behind him, fastened the rope to his hands, and kicked the stool out from under him. So there he hung, in pain, until they finally cut him down.

"The odor from the camp was in our hair, our clothes. We bathed and we bathed and we still had the odor. We finally burned our clothes! I show my pictures to people, and they are amazed at how anybody could do such things. I have two boys, and they know about it, but my wife won't look at the pictures. She says they're too horrible. All we can do is hope it'll never happen again."

JOEL GLOTTER

WITNESS TO THE LIBERATION OF ORHRDRUF

As Joel Glotter's division looked on, General Eisenhower inspected Ohrdruf, saying,"I made the visit deliberately, in order to be in position to give first hand evidence of these things if ever, in the future, there develops a tendency to charge these allegations to 'propaganda'."

Almost 400,000 Minnesotans served in the United States Armed Forces during World War ll. Nearly 8000 died in the service of their country. Like all

Minnesotans, the Jewish community proudly defended American freedom in the European and Pacific theatres. Minnesota Jews received hundreds of decorations for bravery in combat. Along with their fellow Minnesotans, they witnessed the horrors of the war which included the crimes uncovered at the liberation of concentration camps in Germany, Austria and Czechoslovakia.

The future lay unknown to Joel Glotter as he graduated from Minneapolis West High School in the spring of 1943. Like many of his friends, he loved sports—playing football, basketball and baseball—but still found time to track World War II events listening to Edward R. Murrow and Walter Winchell. Joel entered the armed services in an engineering program in Los Angeles, but eventually was moved into the infantry, where he began a journey which would take him across the United States, across the Atlantic and into combat in Europe.

Joel went to Army boot camp in Alabama. He recalled the row upon row of barracks, as the Army was training huge numbers of inductees for combat. This manpower was keenly needed as the United States was fighting the Axis on two fronts stretching thousands of miles a great distance from American shores.

By the time Joel joined his unit—the 89th infantry division—in Europe in December, 1944, the Germans had launched their surprise offensive which became the Battle of the Bulge, seeking to split the allied forces in two by recapturing the crucial Belgian port at Antwerp.

Through savage combat in the bitterly cold winter of December 1944 and January 1945, the American forces decisively defeated the Germans, at great cost. But new horrors demonstrating a different form of savagery awaited some GIs in the late winter and spring of 1945 in Germany, Austria and Czechoslovakia.

Crossing the Rhine in plywood boats under machine gun fire, Joel and the 89th Infantry Division advanced through Germany in March and April 1945. In early April, the division came upon the Ohrdruf concentration camp, a sub-camp of Buchenwald. At Ohrdruf, Joel described witnessing the depravity of the Third Reich as slave laborers—about two thirds of whom were Jews as well as prisoners from all over Europe—were worked to death expanding an underground communication center for Hitler. Joel saw bodies stacked in pyramids ready for burning, which the Germans had been attempting to destroy as evidence. Joel remembered the horrible stench and the piles of ash and bone. He remembered that the American soldiers—despite being hardened by combat—were stunned.

He remembers American officers forcing German civilians from nearby towns to visit the Ohrdruf camp, all denying they knew of its existence. Joel's unit remained for two to three weeks near Ohrdruf. He remembered the famous visit of General Eisenhower to the camp on April 12, 1945. Joining Eisenhower were General Omar Bradley and Lt. General George Patton.

Joel Glotter

Eisenhower inspected Ohrdruf saying, "I made the visit deliberately, in order to be in position to give first hand evidence of these things if ever, in the future, there develops a tendency to charge these allegations to 'propaganda'". As with these generals and hundreds of American soldiers, Joel was a witness. to the German crimes against humanity.

On May 8, as the 89th Infantry Division was advancing on the southern German cities of Stollberg, Lossritz and Aue, the war ended. Joel recalled the division newspaper, the *Rolling W*, declaring, "WAR ENDS."

After the unconditional surrender of Germany, the 89th Division was assigned guard duty for displaced persons camps, hospitals, laboratories and railroad bridges. At Camp Lucky Strike in the LeHavre area of France, the division assisted in the processing of 80,000 prisoners of war.

With the demobilization of the 89th Division, Joel sailed home in the fall of 1945. His father and uncle met him in New York City and they drove home to Minneapolis. Joel enrolled at the University of Minnesota under the GI Bill and received a degree in mathematics and architecture. He went to work as an architect for Liebenberg & Kaplan a firm famous for designing movie theatres. Joel, who had witnessed the medical condition of survivors at the Ohrdruf concentration camp, developed an expertise designing hospitals, working on the Minneapolis Veterans Administration, Hennepin County Medical Center, North Memorial and an addition to Mount Sinai Hospital.

Joel married Joanne Franer in 1952; Joanne died in June 2016. Their children Mark and Toni both married and live in Minneapolis. Joel has a grandson who serves in the Israel Defense Forces and is the father of Joel's first great-grandchild.

ARTHUR L. JOHNSON

WITNESS TO THE LIBERATION OF BUCHENWALD

"Buchenwald was almost unspeakable. Seeing those prisoners' faces—if there was ever a reason for a 'just' war, this was it!"

Arthur L. Johnson graduated college in June 1941, was drafted in October, and landed in Normandy on D-Day plus 12. His company handled 200,000 tons of ammunition in some of the heaviest fighting of the European war.

"Our company was backing up the First Army during the Battle of the Bulge," said Arthur. "We got shot up and our ammunition dump got blown up and we had casualties, but we came out relatively lucky.

"Buchenwald was a shocker. Here were the Germans, civilized people, and the reports in "Stars and Stripes" were almost unspeakable. People dying like flies and piled like cordwood because the Germans ran out of fuel to run the furnace to incinerate the bodies. General Eisenhower wanted the world to see this, so reporters and civilians came from Washington and other places, and it was open for us to see, too.

"Many prisoners were still there when we arrived. They were too weak to leave, and there was no place for them to go before the war finished. There were gaunt faces and sunken eye sockets, people who were emaciated, but they had smiles on their faces. They had hope.

"Many were still wearing their striped prison uniforms, others had picked up parts of American uniforms. Some who spoke English told me about the filth and stench, and one little spigot for a water fountain for a thousand men. One bathroom, dysentery rampant, no food. Many crawled under dead bodies to keep warm, six or eight of them in one little cubicle. Sitting and talking to them, we felt almost numb.

"Then we saw the crematorium. Maybe 150 feet square, a wall around it five or six feet high, brick. When I got there the bodies were gone, but the stench of dead human flesh was still permeating the area.

"A guy took us through and described what the Germans did to the prisoners. They took the dead bodies and the people who were dying or too weak to work, and dumped them all down a hole. People down in the hole would put them up on hooks in the wall, just like sides of beef, hanging the bodies up on these hooks until they were ready to burn them. I still remember going through that L-shaped building with the hooks on the wall like meat hooks. They had room for maybe forty or fifty bodies in this area—efficient. They had whitewashed the walls after liberation, but you could still see on the walls the human bloodstains from the shoulder blades, buttocks, and heels, from people's bodies dripping blood!

"Then they showed us the elevators that would take the bodies efficiently from the basement area up to the incinerator level. And then they'd take the ashes out of the ovens and maybe send a letter to the family that so-and-so had died, and that for a small fee they'd ship them in an urn to the family. The urns were still there, where they would put the ashes and sell them to the families. The image of those furnaces, that building, still haunts me.

"I remember touring the commandant's house, where his wife, the 'bitch of Buchenwald,' Ilse Koch, got strange, morbid satisfaction making lampshades out of human skin because they had interesting tattoos on them. I saw it with my own eyes! And at the same time there were phonograph records in the room—Beethoven, Brahms, Wagner.

"It still puzzles me that here was Buchenwald, just ten or fifteen miles from Weimar, and all these people in Weimar claimed they didn't know anything about what was going on. The paradox of Germany—with its cultural achievements, its Nobel Prize winners, playing Beethoven or Mozart while this kind of barbarity was going on.

"Some people say the Holocaust is a hoax. But I was there. I saw Buchenwald with my own eyes."

WILLIAM LANDGREN

WITNESS TO THE LIBERATION OF DACHAU

"I was used to seeing dead soldiers in battle, but then I saw a little girl's head sticking out, with the rest of the bodies around it, and it hit me how they must have suffered."

Drafted at age twenty-five, Bill Landgren went overseas in 1943. He was assigned to the 45th Division just before the amphibious landing at Anzio. The 45th was in combat for 511 days in Italy, France, and Germany.

"I graduated in agronomy at Iowa State and took ROTC for two years, field artillery," said Bill. "When I was drafted I thought, 'It's a cinch I'll get into field artillery.' Then the sergeant says, 'You're in the infantry now, brother.' I was a 'ninety-day wonder'—graduated Officers' Candidate School as a second lieutenant in ninety days. I was commander of a machine gun platoon.

"Going into Munich, I followed the train track into Dachau, behind our riflemen. I'd picked up an old camera and fifteen or twenty rolls of film, so I got a lot of pictures. Here they are, a cluster of German guards and their dogs, dead, and more than forty coal cars and enclosed boxcars, full of dead. Outside the crematorium was a huge pile of bodies, twice the size of my living room, and you can see how thin they were, just skeletons, and they'd started to deteriorate.

"The town of Dachau was about two or three miles away, and of course the people in the town claimed they didn't know what was going on. So we Americans brought them out, made them bring their wagons and their horses, made them walk through town with the bodies, and then bury them in a mass grave outside of town. I have a picture of a guy using ice tongs to pick up those bodies because they were so badly decomposed.

"I sent the film to my mother and father. They didn't know what was on it, and they took it down to the photographer and told him to develop them. When the photographer saw what they were, he made a display in his window. My mother wouldn't even look at them.

Former prisoners and camp guards at Dachau take corpses to crematorium. April, 1945
Photo by William Landgren

"I knew the photo album was up in the attic, and then I got to thinking about it, and years later I got it down. I'd show it to people, our friends, but I never showed the pictures to my kids. My wife and I took a trip to Germany, and we had a German woman taking us on a tour of Munich. I said, 'I'd like to go to Dachau, where the concentration camp was. I was there during the war.'

"'Nothing's there,' she said, 'You're wasting your time. It's all gone.' Back home, my son's wife said, 'What do you mean there's nothing there? They've got the barracks, there's a museum! Here are pictures!'"

WITNESSES TO THE HOLOCAUST

DR. WILLIAM McCONAHEY

MEDICAL OFFICER AT FLOSSENBURG

"I don't think I could have understood what it was like to be there without having actually been there. The hopelessness of it, no way out. Only torture, only misery, only starvation, and finally death."

As a surgeon with the 337th Infantry, Dr. William McConahey was in charge of a front-line first aid station.

"We were on the 'first team,' which meant we went in at Utah Beach on D-Day plus 2," said Dr. McConahey. "I marched my men inland to rendezvous with paratroopers who had jumped ahead of us, and we dug foxholes for our first night on shore. The next day we got our jeeps in, with our medical equipment.

"I was as far forward as medical officers got, about a mile behind the front lines, or less We had the Red Cross front and back on our helmets, on both arms, and on our jeeps. The German army respected the Red Crosses—usually.

"I had about fifteen surgical and medical technicians and a couple of jeep drivers. Our job was to get the wounded out of the front lines, splint bones, stop bleeding, dress wounds, stop shock, stop pain, and get them back where they could get surgery, suturing, more care. I'd have to use lights at night, so I'd set up in a house or barn or in an orchard. We would be in a position maybe two or three days, maybe two or three hours. We could close up and hop in a jeep and be gone in ten minutes!

"As we moved into Germany we started hearing about the concentration camps at army briefings. April 23 our division liberated Flossenburg, and I went in there the next day. Flossenburg had held 15,000 prisoners but there were only about 1,500 left. The German guards had marched out about 13,000 toward Dachau, to get away from our advancing army. It was a very poignant, sad-looking road because they'd been marched out carrying a blanket or maybe a jacket, but they were too weak to carry things, and they'd dropped them along the way.

"A few very emaciated prisoners were wandering around in blue-and-white striped prison garb. My jeep driver spoke German, so he had conversations with many of the prisoners. They were from all over Europe— Poles, Russians, Czechs, French, Belgians, Spaniards. They had a lot of Jewish people there, of course, but many were political prisoners, from the Underground, or just people picked up by the Gestapo because they thought they were anti-Hitler. They all bore the scars of beatings and being knocked around.

"The camp was laid out in very neat barracks style, with two big barbed wire fences around it. Running through it was a little railroad with a little pushcart like you see in coal mines, pushed by hand, to haul bodies to the crematory. Three inmates, pretty much zombies, were still burning bodies in the crematorium because prisoners were still dying left and right, and for sanitation they had to do something! About sixteen corpses were lined up to be burned. They were just skin and bone, each one weighing about forty pounds, I'd guess, because you could pick them up with one hand. One fellow opened the furnace door, and there were a couple of bodies in there, burning.

"We saw the beautiful houses where the S.S. guards lived with their women. Then I walked into the barracks, very drab and cold, with three tiers of bunks on each side. Nothing but boards—no mattresses, no straw, nothing. Each bunk was big enough for one, but they said three had slept there every night.

"I visited the 'hospital' where they brought prisoners to die. They'd put them on the bare wooden floor with straw on it, and they'd lie there in their own excrement and vomit until they died. Some prisoners, their spirits broken, were just shells. They'd lost the will to live. Some were so close to death you couldn't feed them because they hadn't eaten for so long their stomachs were atrophied, and if they ate, they vomited and bloated and obstructed. We tried to get them back on small feedings very slowly, over a period of weeks, but we couldn't save most of them. We felt terrible. They were dying before our eyes, and there was nothing we could do.

"After the war ended, we drove to Dachau one day. Dachau was much bigger than Flossenburg. Again, we toured the barracks and saw the crematories, six big ovens. Outside were thousands of jars stacked up, the charred bones and ashes of people who had been burned there. I was told they used these ashes for fertilizing the gardens. We saw the whipping posts, the torture chambers. It was degradation and terror and horror and suffering, just like Flossenburg, only on a bigger scale.

"It was those concentration camps that made us realize what we were fighting for. We really felt it was a holy crusade to wipe out that diabolical regime. We may have sadistic psychopaths in this country who could do what the S.S. did in Germany, but Hitler gave them a rank, a uniform, a purpose and a mission, and encouraged them.

"The infantry medical corps was not like 'M.A.S.H.' or the movies. Unless you were there, in combat and fighting the battle, crawling on your belly under machine gun fire, and digging a foxhole in the rain and getting shelled, you can't understand what it was like.

"The war marked me for life. I realized that making a lot of money or being a big shot wasn't as important as doing something worthwhile, being a good person was what counted."

KAY BONNER NEE

WITNESS TO THE LIBERATION OF BUCHENWALD

"I would rather not talk about Buchenwald, but our children must know that this was real, it happened. If they don't know, how can they be instruments of peace? How can they help us to make sure that it never happens again?"

In 1943 Kay Bonner went to England as an entertainer attached to Special Services, assigned to the Fifth Corps of the First Army. Kay and her partner were the first women to land in Normandy after D-Day.

"If you had the ability to sing, dance, do funny sayings, and play a musical instrument, and could learn to drive a two-ton truck, you could work with Special Services," said Kay. "Our assignment was to entertain where the big stars couldn't go. They needed stages and equipment; we needed nothing but our truck. It had a piano, a microphone, and a side that let down to make a stage.

Kay Bonner Nee

"We performed while soldiers watched from their foxholes, and V-1 rockets buzzed overhead. When the buzzing stopped, it meant the rocket was going to land, and you'd better head for cover— fast! At Eupen, German parachutists were landing and we were being strafed, and finally we left in the dark, with tracer bullets the only light we had to see by. Katie Cullen, the girl with me, was killed.

"When we came to Buchenwald, most of the Germans had fled. Their goal had been to eliminate all their prisoners and burn their remains, so that when the Americans arrived there would be an empty camp. But there was not enough time. As I entered the camp, I was overcome with the horrible stench of still-burning flesh and hair, decaying bodies, and unsanitary conditions. I remember thinking 'they can take photographs, they can write about Buchenwald, but it will be impossible to describe the terrible odor.'

"Most of the prisoners were Jews, but the camp also contained political prisoners of many nationalities. There was a Belgian general whose friends brought his old uniform and put it on him. The uniform just hung, because there was nothing left of him but skin and bones, and he was not going to survive. But his friends were marching him along, holding him up, and tears of happiness were streaming down his face.

"Inside the camp office the furnishings were lavish. It was here that the wife of the commander, known as the 'bitch of Buchenwald,' displayed her lampshades made from the tattooed skin of prisoners. Outside the office were contraptions on which they hung prisoners by first tying their hands behind their backs, and then attaching rope to the hands and pulling them backwards and upwards to hang from the posts. A prisoner did not have to hang very long before the arms were detached from their sockets.

"At the right as you entered the camp, were the crematoriums. The ovens were still smoking, with half-burned bodies inside. Beside the ovens were the emaciated bodies of prisoners they had not had time to burn, naked men and women together, stacked as you would stack your fireplace wood. I remember thinking, 'No one will believe this, I must take pictures.' But my hands, my whole body, was shaking so that I jammed the shutter and dropped the camera.

"These emaciated, skeletal figures were real people, human beings. They had all lived and breathed and talked and loved, as is the right of every human. To end in the ovens, stacked like cordwood on the ground or piled in a cart, seemed the most inhuman of ends to a human life. Not far from the ovens was a cement torture chamber. The walls were three feet thick to muffle the screams. There was a drain in the cement floor so they could hose away the blood. On the walls were great meat hooks where they hung prisoners like chunks of beef until they died. The prisoner who was pointing out these instruments of torture told me that his wife and two sons had died on the hooks.

"Further down from the torture chamber, to the left were the barracks. Wooden beds with no mattresses reached to the ceiling. And the last barracks contained people so ill, so emaciated, that they were more dead than alive. It was impossible even to tell whether these people were old or young. They were living dead, so starved and mistreated they couldn't even remember where they came from.

"Some were still conscious enough to know that liberation had come. And then I, this good American, out of ignorance, did the worst thing I could have. I gave them all the food I had, chocolate bars and cheese and K-rations, concentrated food, richer by far than regular food. When the medics came, they fed them gruel made of dried potatoes and watery powdered milk. But I had no experience, no training in medicine, and it did not occur to me that the rich food would be impossible for people who had been starved for so long to digest.

"The next day we brought the townspeople out to Buchenwald, and we showed them through the camp. 'You did this,' we told them. And the people answered, 'No, not us, it was Hitler.' 'You allowed it to happen,' we said. 'You are responsible.' They said, 'No, no. We didn't even know the camp was here.' But the prisoners said they had been taken into town to fix roads and repair buildings. They said villagers had taunted them and thrown stones. How could they not know the camp was there?

"I looked into the eyes of death in these prisoners, and I wondered what their lives had been like before Buchenwald. I hugged and kissed them, and cried with them, and murmured to them in a language most did not understand. And I watched them die. One person's hand turned stiff as I held it.

"I was in Buchenwald for about a week-and-a-half, and then the army was moving on and I had to go with them. Later I used to see people from the camps, carrying little bags over their shoulders or pushing a two-wheeler cart they had found. And the thing I almost couldn't stand was that they didn't know they were going back to towns that had been blown away, to homes that no longer existed, to family who had disappeared.

"When I was growing up, my ambitions were to have a reasonable amount of money and a lot of fun. But this unbelievable experience changed my values, my attitude, my whole life. I had not been politically active or even aware before the war, but I became so afterwards. And whenever I feel that one person cannot do much, or that what I'm doing is not important or not having any effect, I remember the Germans saying, 'No, we are not responsible,' and our answer, 'Yes, you are. You allowed it to happen.'"

WITNESS TO THE LIBERATION OF DACHAU

"Many times when I was lying in a foxhole, or sweating out an artillery barrage, or lying in the rain pinned down by enemy fire, I asked myself, 'Why am I here?' After what I saw at Dachau, I had the answer."

Leonard Parker enlisted in the army at age nineteen. He and his squad were scouting ahead of their unit when they came to a small town named Dachau. Parker knew Yiddish, so he could talk with Dachau prisoners about their experiences.

"I enlisted in the army for no good reason, except I thought it would be an adventure," said Leonard. "I was fourteen months in combat, ending up a tech sergeant in charge of a platoon. My platoon was out in front when we came upon this little town not far from Munich. The sign said 'Dachau.'

"As we were approaching the town, there was a terrible odor. German civilians were looting the stores, and no one seemed to be paying attention that we were coming through. There was no evidence of German soldiers. The odor was coming from a railroad siding where there were flat cars loaded with bodies. There were young children and women and men, machine-gunned to death by the S.S. because they couldn't be taken along by the retreating Nazis. Those bodies had been lying out there in the sun for three days, and the stink was awful.

"When we got to the far side of town we saw stone walls, with barbed wire and metal fencing. We could see buildings through the wire. We stopped because we didn't know what to expect, and the commanding officer sent me, with one squad of my people, to see what was going on. As we approached the camp, out of the gate very timidly came three prisoners dressed in blue-and-white striped prisoner clothes with prisoner caps, so thin they looked like sticks. Then the first one yelled at me in English, 'Boy, are we glad to see you!' He was a U.S. Army captain, who had parachuted into France on a secret mission and been captured! Then a flood of human skeletons came out of the gates. The seven of us were just surrounded by these prisoners and they grabbed our hands and kissed them, many of them crying in Yiddish, 'Thank God, you've come to set us free!' These women, children, and men were crying with joy, half mad with happiness. Many of us had eyes overflowing with tears, too.

"When I started answering them in Yiddish, they just went crazy, and then I started to sing for them, 'My Yiddische Mama,' and they're all crying, and I'm crying. They couldn't believe there were Jewish soldiers in the American army, and when I told them I was an officer one asked if I would write my Jewish name for him on a piece of paper. Soon I was scribbling it for them all, on dirty scraps of paper that appeared in their hands like magic, as a souvenir from the American Jewish soldier.

"We spent about an hour talking to them, listening to countless stories about the cruelty of the Nazis. I reported what was going on to our battalion commander, and we guarded the camp for three hours, until the American military government moved in to take over.

"We went through where they gassed people, and we saw and smelled the furnace room, giant ovens with pieces of bones and ash still in them. We went through barracks full of people who were too sick and too weak to get up. They were just lying there dying, in incredible filth. We took no German prisoners that day. All that we captured, maybe 50 S.S., we killed.

"I had my squad in a house in the city of Dachau, and we asked the lady who owned the house, 'Didn't you know this was going on?' 'Oh, no.' Their insistence that they didn't know what was going on was a lie."

LARRY TILLEMANS

CLERK-STENOGRAPHER, NUREMBERG TRIALS

Larry Tillemans of St. Joseph, Minnesota, was a clerk-stenographer with the United States Third Army assigned to the Nuremberg and Dachau war crimes trials. As part of the American prosecution team for Nuremberg, he worked with a team which typed over 200,000 affidavits from victims of Nazism. He has vivid recollections of defendants Herman Goering and Albert Speer and he described the lead prosecutor, Justice Robert Jackson as "the most brilliant man I ever heard talk."

Born in Minneota, Minnesota in 1926, Larry Tillemans was part of a large Dutch-American Family. Of the nine siblings, five were born in Holland and four were born in the United States, including Larry. Larry's father was a hog buyer. Southwest Minnesota in the 1930's was heavily agricultural, with strong connections to Europe, particularly to Holland and Belgium. The family had relatives who endured the German occupation of Holland from 1940 to 1944.

Larry grew up in Minneota with a population of about 900. He was educated in public and parochial schools and loved basketball; he was shooting baskets on a basket hanging from the barn when he heard the news of Pearl Harbor. His family was devoted to scouting. He and two brothers were Eagle Scouts. A picture of the three brothers, their father and the scout master appeared in "Boys Life" magazine in 1941. A patriotic family, two of Larry's brothers served in the southwest Pacific in the Second World War.

Minneota was deeply patriotic. The four corner houses, including the Tillemans', had eleven family members in the United States armed services in the Second World War. One was killed in action and another lost both legs in combat. Seventy five percent of the boys in Larry's high school class served in the Second World War. "Sixteen million Americans served in the armed forces in the Second World War," noted Larry, with a million volunteering for service on December 8, 1941, after the invasion of Pearl Harbor.

The foundation for Larry's service with the American prosecution team at Nuremberg was laid at Minneota High School. He was the only boy in a typing class of 15 students. He enlisted in the Army in 1944 and was inducted at Fort Snelling. He took his basic training in Texas, and qualified for the Signal Corps by virtue of his typing skills.

Arriving in LeHavre, France, in March, 1945, he joined the American prosecution team in 1945. He was assigned to a clerk/stenographer pool of 30–40 with the Third Army. From his experience typing affidavits and from watching a few sessions of the trial, he learned about what he called "the horrors of the camps." He has vivid recollections of defendants Herman Goering and Albert Speer and he described the lead American prosecutor, Justice Robert Jackson, as "the most brilliant man I ever heard talk."

Forty five years later, Larry was inspired to begin talking about his Nuremberg war crimes trial experience as well as his view of the dangers of Nazism. After this life-changing experience, he pledged to give back to the community by teaching about the Nuremberg Trials. He estimated he has given over 400 talks to schools, churches, prisons and civic groups. "Kids can't get enough of it" and appreciate "living history," said Larry.

AFFIDAVIT: Permit papers needed by refugees to emigrate to the United States; required to be signed by a U.S. citizen who guaranteed that the refugee would not need public assistance.

ALIYAH: To emigrate to Palestine or Israel; literally in Hebrew "going up."

ALIYAH BET: Hebrew name for illegal immigration of Jews to Palestine during the Hitler era.

ARMBAND: Jews under Nazi rule were often required to wear a yellow or white armband with a six-pointed Star of David.

ARYAN, ARYANIZED: Linguistic term that symbolized the myth of German superiority; a Caucasian gentile, especially one of Nordic stock; non-Jewish, having no Jewish ancestors.

BREICHAH: Underground route of escape to Palestine after the war.

BRITISH MANDATE: Policy to deny permission to most would-be emigrants to Israel.

BUND, BUNDISTS: Yiddish-speaking Socialist group.

CHILDREN'S TRANSPORTS: Evacuation of Jewish children during the 1930s, mostly from Germany, to England, the United States, Argentina, Brazil, and other countries; organized by the refugee organization HIAS and the Joint Distribution Committee (JDC).

CONCENTRATION CAMP: Organized in early 1930s for "preventive detention" of political opponents of the Nazi regime. Later used for Jews, Romani, homosexuals, prisoners of war, members of the Resistance, and as a source for forced labor and human subjects for medical experiments by S.S. doctors.

COSSACKS: Peasant soldiers in Ukraine and other parts of Russian Empire, part of Czar's military forces; associated with attacks on Jews known as "pogroms."

DISPLACED PERSONS CAMPS (D.P. CAMPS): When World War II ended, there were an estimated thirty million displaced persons in Europe including many Holocaust survivors. D.P.s included slave laborers, political and other prisoners, and people who had been forcibly removed from their homes, who had fled, or whose homes or cities had been destroyed. The Allies set up displaced persons camps to provide temporary housing, food, and other support services.

EICHMANN, ADOLPH: Head of the Jewish Office of the Gestapo; planned and organized the destruction of Europe's Jews.

EINSATZKOMMANDOS: Special military units recruited by Hitler and Himmler to exterminate the Russian Jewish population and Communist leaders; killed an estimated two million Jews, often forcing them to dig their own maS.S. graves and then mowing them down with machine gun fire.

THE FORWARD (JEWISH DAILY FORWARD): American Yiddish-language newspaper with nationwide circulation, established in New York City in 1897; became a contact point for survivors and relatives after World War II.

GERMAN SOCIALISTS: Political organization that became the basis for the Nazi party.

GESTAPO: Secret police organized by the Nazis.

GHETTO: A compulsory area of residence for Jews, in a prescribed section of a city, often surrounded by walls or barbed wire.

GPU: Russian secret police, organized after the 1917 Revolution; in 1934 its functions were transferred to the NKVD, which was also responsible for forced labor camps.

GYMNASIUM: European equivalent of American high school.

HACHSHERAH: "Training farms" in Europe and the United States during 1930s for young city dwellers planning to emigrate to Palestine.

HAGANAH: Underground Jewish defense organization in Palestine established to protect Jewish life and property against attack by Arabs; literally "defense" in Hebrew.

HASHOMER HATZAIR: Jewish Socialist organization for young people,

HASIDIM, HASIDIC (ALSO CHASIDIM, CHASIDIC): A hasid is a member of a Jewish sect founded in Poland, known for piety as well as joy and mysticism. Hasidic is the adjective, hasidim is the plural.

HIAS (HEBREW SHELTERING AND IMMIGRANT AID SOCIETY): International aid organization established in the United States in 1884.

HIGH HOLIDAYS: The Jewish New Year; includes the holidays of Rosh

Hashanah and Yom Kippur, the Day of Atonement, a fast day.

HILFSVEREIN (HILFSVEREIN DER DEUTSCHEN JUDEN): The German Jewish Relief Association; a German government-sponsored agency that helped Jews emigrate from Germany before WWII; disbanded in 1939.

HITLER YOUTH: Militaristic Nazi-oriented youth organization emphasizing hiking, camping, and sports, but also precision marching, war games, political indoctrination and discipline.

IRON CROSS: German military decoration; many German Jews won the Iron CroS.S. fighting for Germany during World War I.

IRON GUARD: Romanian political party that attacked Jews.

JEWISH FAMILY AND CHILDREN'S SERVICE (JFCS,JFS): Local community organizations in the United States that helped arriving refugees find housing, jobs, English lessons, and so on.

JEWISH NATIONAL FUND (JNF): International organization for buying and planting trees in Israel; founded by Theodor Herzl.

JOINT DISTRIBUTION COMMITTEE (JDC, THE JOINT): Founded 1914 to provide emergency aid for war victims in Europe.

JUDENFREI: German for "free of Jews," it was a goal of Nazi Germany to make Germany Judenfrei.

JUDENRAT: Jewish Council; originally elected by members of a Jewish community but later by the Nazis, to administer affairs of the Jewish community. Under the Nazis, the Judenrat was forced to manage the ghetto and enforce Nazi edicts.

KAPO: Concentration camp inmate chosen by the Nazis to oversee other inmates; some kapos were Jews.

KEHILLA: Jewish community council.

KIBBUTZ: A cooperative agricultural community in Israel with all members sharing the work and sharing equally in profits.

KOSHER: Food prepared and eaten according to Jewish dietary laws in which animals and poultry are inspected for cleanlineS.S. and health and humanely slaughtered. Pork and shellfish are forbidden. Meat and dairy products cannot be served at the same meal.

KRISTALLNACHT: A maS.S. orchestrated attack Jewish communities in

Germany and Austria on November 9, 1938, literally "Night of the Broken Glass." Anti-Jewish riots instigated by the Nazis in one night, resulting in 20,000 Jews arrested and sent to concentration camps, hundreds killed, 101 synagogues burned, and 7,500 Jewish-owned businesses looted and destroyed.

LABOR CAMP: Prison camps where Jews and other prisoners of the Nazis were forced to work as slave laborers in factories on road construction, etc.

LIQUIDATION: Systematic maS.S. killing of all or most of the residents of a city, town, ghetto, or concentration camp.

MATZAH: Unleavened, cracker-like bread eaten during the eight days of Passover.

MEIN KAMPF: Book written by Adolf Hitler, proclaiming his beliefs, which became the Nazi credo.

MELAMED: Hebrew word for teacher.

MENGELE, DR. JOSEF: Notorious S.S. captain at Auschwitz who used Jews in sadistic medical experiments.

MEZUZAH: A ritual item, a mezuzah is a small case containing a Hebrew prayer; it is nailed to the upper part of the right doorpost in a Jewish home.

MUSSULMEN: People who have lost the look of a human being; human skeletons whose minds are no longer functioning. Dazed concentration camp inmates were referred to by this German word.

MAGEN DAVID: Six-pointed Star of David, symbol of the Jewish people. (See Star of David).

NAZI: Abbreviation for the German National Socialist Workers' Party.

NKVD: Soviet secret police. They also supervised forced labor camps in the Soviet Union during WWII.

ORTHODOX: Observant Jews.

PALESTINE: Historically, the region on the eastern shore of the Mediterranean, comprising parts of modern Israel, Jordan, and Egypt. During World War I the British gained control of what was then known as Palestine from Turkey and continued to govern it under a mandate from the League of Nations until parts of Palestine became The State of Israel by United Nations vote in 1948.

PARTISANS: Underground resistance groups, both Jewish and non-Jewish, in southern and eastern Europe, mainly operating in forests of the Ukraine, Poland, and Lithuania, who fought the Nazis by sabotage and other methods.

PASSOVER: Eight-day spring festival of freedom, celebrating the biblical exodus of the Jews from slavery in Egypt.

PEOPLE OF THE BOOK: Jews are sometimes referred to in this way because Judaism is based on the first five books of the Bible ("the book").

POGROMS: Systematic massacres and murderous attacks on Jews; some of the worst took place in Russia in the nineteenth and early twentieth centuries, but there were some pogroms in Poland and other countries even after World War II.

QUOTAS: Restrictions enacted by the United States in 1921 and 1924 (the Johnson Act) limiting U.S. immigration, especially from Eastern Europe, to small percentages of those nationalities already resident in the United States. The U.S. State Department used quotas and red tape to prevent Jews from immigrating to the United States during the 1930s. Despite the flood of applicants, many quotas went unfilled.

RED CROS.S. "BRIEF": During World War II the International Red CroS.S. helped to deliver short messages ("Brief" is German for letter) between people in Germany and Austria and their relatives who had escaped.

(THE) RESISTANCE: Organized underground and guerilla opposition to the German occupiers.

RIGHTEOUS GENTILES: Non-Jews who risked their lives to save Jews during the Nazi era.

ROSH HASHANAH: The Jewish New Year which comes in September or early October; literally Hebrew for "the head of the year."

S.A. ("STURM ABTEILUNG" OR STORM TROOPERS): German organization, begun secretly, to supplement the small regular army Germany was allowed under the Treaty of Versailles after WWI.

SCHINDLER, OSKAR: Wealthy German industrialist who risked his life during the Hitler era to save Jews who worked for him in his factory at Cracow-Plaschau and later in Germany.

SELECTION: ProceS.S. in which groups of prisoners in labor camps or concentration camps were separated into two groups; strong, youthful people were saved for work or medical experiments, and most children, old people, pregnant women, and people who appeared sick or weak were "selected" to be killed immediately.

SHABBOS: Yiddish word for Sabbath, the day of rest.

SHOCHET: Man trained and authorized by the Jewish community to slaughter poultry and animals in accordance with dietary laws of Kashrut.

SHOFAR: Ritual ram's horn blown on the Jewish high Holidays of Rosh Hashanah and Yom Kippur.

SHTETL: Small town or village in Eastern Europe, literally "little town" in Yiddish.

SIDE CURLS: Also known as "payes" (Yiddish) or "payot" (Hebrew). Earlocks or untrimmed sideburns worn by some Orthodox Jewish men and boys.

S.S.: Black-shirted troops organized as Hitler's personal bodyguard, later assigned to organize and staff the concentration camps; "Schutz Staffeln" in German.

STAR OF DAVID: Six-pointed star, also known as Mogen Dovid (Yiddish) or Magen David (Hebrew), symbol of the biblical King David; adopted by Zionists as the Jewish national symbol.

SWASTIKA: Ancient symbol used as a religious emblem to ward off evil spirits but adopted by Hitler as the symbol of the Nazis.

THIRD REICH: The First Reich (Empire) was the Holy Roman Empire; the Second Reich included the German Empire (1871-1919) and the post-World War I Weimar Republic (1919-33); the Third Reich was the Nazi state under Adolf Hitler, (1933-45).

TORAH: First five books of the Bible (Five Books of Moses), the ritual Torah is handwritten in Hebrew on a parchment scroll.

UNRRA (UNITED NATIONS RELIEF AND REHABILITATION ADMINISTRATION): Organized in November 1943 by forty-three nations to provide food, clothing, medical supplies, and other assistance to refugees.

V-E DAY: Victory in Europe Day, May 8, 1945, the day Germany surrendered.

VOLKSDEUTSCH: People of German descent.

WALLENBERG, RAOUL: Swedish diplomat who saved many Hungarian Jews by arranging false passports and establishing "safe houses" in Budapest. Wehrmacht German army.

WEIMAR REPUBLIC: German democratic government during the years 1919-33.

YAD VASHEM: Holocaust Memorial Museum in Jerusalem.

YELLOW STAR: Jews in Nazi-occupied countries were forced to wear an identifying armband with the six-pointed Star of David or to sew a yellow fabric star on their clothing. In some countries, the stars were blue on white.

YIDDISH: Language spoken by Eastern European Jews with many German-based words but written with Hebrew letters.

YOM KIPPUR: The Day of Atonement, a fast day and the most important holiday of the Jewish year.

YOUTH ALIYAH: Organization that brought survivor children from Europe to Palestine after the Holocaust and cared for them.

ZIONISM: Zionist Movement for Jewish homeland, dating from the First Zionist International Congress, convened by Theodor Herzl on August 28, 1897, in Basel, Switzerland.

ZLOTY: Polish monetary unit.